THE

Art of Teaching School.

A MANUAL OF SUGGESTIONS

FOR THE USE OF

TEACHERS AND SCHOOL AUTHORITIES, SUPERINTENDENTS, CONTROLLERS, DIRECTORS, TRUSTEES AND PATRONS OF PUBLIC SCHOOLS AND HIGHER INSTITUTIONS OF LEARNING.

HOW TO ESTABLISH, ORGANIZE, GOVERN AND TEACH SCHOOLS OF ALL GRADES, AND WHAT TO TEACH.

By J. R. SYPHER,
Author of "History of Pennsylvania," "History of New Jersey," "American Popular Speaker," etc.

NEW EDITION.

PHILADELPHIA:
J. M. STODDART & CO.
J. A. BANCROFT & CO.
CHICAGO AND INDIANAPOLIS:
A. H. ANDREWS & CO.
ST. LOUIS:
WESTERN PUBLISHING AND SCHOOL FURNISHING CO.

WESTCOTT & THOMSON,
Stereotypers and Electrotypers, Philada.

SHERMAN & CO.,
Printers, Phila.

PREFACE.

THE State establishes public schools for the economical education of youth, in the elementary departments of useful knowledge. These schools are supported by a general tax, and are for the use of all the people. Whenever, by systems of organization, by courses of study or by methods of instruction, their usefulness is impaired, the object of the State is defeated, and the Commonwealth suffers injury. In some portions of the United States this defeat and this injury are already experienced. This book has been written in the belief that its contents will assist those, who are laboring, as school officers, teachers and patrons, to restore the system of public education to its normal life, and to make the public schools serve the ends for which they were established.

PHILADELPHIA, Nov. 29, 1871.

CONTENTS.

CHAPTER I.

CHAPTER II.

CHAPTER III

CHAPTER IV.

CHAPTER V.

CHAPTER VI.

CHAPTER VII.

CHAPTER VIII.

CHAPTER IX.

CHAPTER X.

CHAPTER XI.

CHAPTER XII.

CHAPTER XIII.

CHAPTER XIV.

CHAPTER XV.

CHAPTER XVI.

CHAPTER XVII.

CHAPTER XVIII.

ART OF TEACHING SCHOOL.

CHAPTER I.

EDUCATION.

GENERAL PRINCIPLES.

A SYSTEM of education, to be of practical utility, must be so devised as to secure the harmonious development of all the human faculties, physical and spiritual. The human mind and body are so closely wedded to each other that whatever affects the one for good or evil to a corresponding degree affects the other. It is not necessary to provide an elaborate system of physical training for people so active and stirring as are those who inhabit the United States, but it is essential that a system of intellectual and moral training shall be so constructed and applied as not to obstruct the natural growth and development of the physical powers. The spirit must rule over the body, but that rule must not be oppressive. The body must be held in natural subjection to the spirit, but if by tyranny and oppression the spirit emaciates and enfeebles the body, the effect would be to invoke feebleness and insanity upon itself. The cases in America where harm comes to the body from a too close application to study are exceedingly rare. The tyranny of fashion in dress, the late hours and demoralizing influences of social amusements, the pampering of the appetite and the youthful dissipation consequent upon social usages in good society work irreparable mischief in the young constitution; this is very generally charged as the result of too close application to study in school. The charge is false in every sense. The demand for the relaxation of educational discipline, if granted, would enlarge the opportunities for this social demoralization, and increase the evil results of the pernicious practices to which the ill health of boys and girls is truly attributable.

THE MIND.

The faculties of the mind are comprised in three general divisions—the *Intellect*, the *Sensibility* and the *Will;* that is, the knowing faculties, the feeling faculties and the doing faculties. The logical order is—first, to know; second, to feel; and third, to act. Knowledge precedes emotion; emotion precedes action.

Natural Order of Development.—First in order, then, is the education of the Intellect. The Intellect is developed by the acquisition of knowledge. Knowledge is first acquired, in youth, through the Senses. The first efforts in educating, therefore, should be directed to systematize observation, and the first subjects of study are very naturally the facts in the physical sciences. The innumerable and marvelous questionings in childhood have almost always reference to things seen, felt and heard. He who attempts to teach a child to reason betrays a lamentable ignorance of the order of development of the mental powers. A child will observe, and by processes peculiarly its own will connect facts, and by the operation of Judgment will connect effects with causes, but to endeavor to exercise its mind upon abstractions would be prejudicial to healthful and logical development. From the observation of things the mind gradually rises to the observation of certain qualities belonging to the things observed. Thus Perception is developed. The association of qualities with each other or with a given object gives rise to ideas; these ideas find expression in words; that is, the object is first observed with close interest and attention;

secondly, particular features or properties of the object are observed, and these features or properties are united in the mind as belonging to one object. This unity by which the object and its properties are combined stands in the mind as a representative of the thing observed as a Perception, and may be recalled from the storehouse of Memory by the operation of Recollection, though the thing itself be absent. When a new object is presented, if it in any respect resembles in form or quality the subject of a previous observation, the old is instantly called up and placed in the mind by the side of the new, and this gives rise to association and analysis; each is analyzed to see in what respects it is like and in what it is unlike the other.

Language is first learned by observation, and in every case it is more the result of habit than of analysis. A child imitates the language of its mother; the most persistent efforts of the school-teacher will not be able to overthrow the good or bad results of the every-day practice of the household until the pupil shall have arrived at that age, and shall have attained that degree of culture, which will enable it to distinguish in social life between the correct and the incorrect use of language.

Knowledge that is acquired through the Senses is retained in the Memory, and Recollection is the power by which that which lies in the mind is awakened. Imagination is the power by which the mind holds up before itself the images which are called up by recollection. Understanding is the faculty by which the relations of things to each other are determined. Reason, which is higher than all of these, is the faculty through which the ultimate and universal principles are ascertained. Following this order, which is the order in which these faculties are developed, Memory must be exercised in conjunction with the Senses and Perception. It is the storehouse into which the Perceptive faculties carry all the facts obtained through the Senses. Calling up for inspection the things which are thus stored in the mind gives exercise to the Memory; holding them up to view affords exercise to the Imagination. The Understanding takes up the pictures of the Imagination, receives what Recollection has called up from the Memory, which has been stored by the operation of the Senses, and determines the relations of all the parts to each other as causes and effects. It classifies in accordance with perceived relations. It places facts together as the links in a chain. It discovers that one link hangs upon the other, and that the link which stood as cause for that below it becomes effect for that above it; thus it can follow from the lowest link to the highest, but it can never rise to the ascertaining of the origin of the separate links, or to the comprehension of the power which sustains the whole chain, which seems to hang upon nothing. It is the province of Reason to take up the work where the operations of Judgment end, and to carry the mind from facts to principles, lifting it up to the comprehension of original causation which cannot stand in the relation of effect to any cause.

THE SOURCES OF KNOWLEDGE.

It will thus be observed that there are two sources of knowledge—the Senses and the Reason. Man derives knowledge through the Senses; this is called empirical knowledge—the knowledge of experience. This includes all that we know through the Senses—seeing, hearing, touching, tasting, smelling—and through emotional experiences. Knowledge of which reason is the source is called rational knowledge; ideas of space, of time, of distance, the truths evolved by mathematical calculations, ideas of the absolute and the infinite, are attained through processes of reasoning, and cannot be reached by experience.

METHODS OF ACQUIRING KNOWLEDGE.

There are two methods of dealing with the products of the Senses and of the Reason. Particular phenomena may be taken up and the process be conducted so as to find the general laws, which unite these, into a harmonious system. This is called induction.

Or, a general truth may be presented, and the process will then be to find the original elements which enter into its composition; this process is called deduction. All investigation, therefore, whether for the purpose of acquiring a knowledge of ascertained truths or for undiscovered truths, is either inductive or deductive.

The inductive process is synthetic and the deductive is analytic. By synthesis the parts are constructed into a whole; by analysis the whole is separated into its parts. The naturalist may observe many facts in some department of nature; he may observe the laws which govern these facts, and he may bind all of these into a system of science. This he does by the process of induction, aided by synthesis, or he may observe some general effect, some phenomenon, which stands as a result; he seeks to discover its origin; he divides and subdivides until he reaches simple truths. This is the process of deduction, carried on by analysis.

THE OPERATION OF THE FACULTIES.

By a series of experiments, one suggesting another, the mind proceeds in its search for truth by means of observation, and these same processes, carried on in the higher operations of scientific investigation, had their beginning in smaller and more simple processes in the mind of the child. Associated facts are always attractive to children and readily engage their attention, and it is for this reason that study is most rapid where associated facts, systematically arranged, are presented. The mind thus rises through all the parts of a science, observing at every step the logical order of combination. When knowledge comes in this connected order, its acquisition gives strength to the Memory, because the truths that are learned are so stored away in the mind that the presentation of one induces the recollection of another, and thus innumerable incidents in the range of observation call up long trains of thought. This brings in review before the mind, frequently, in moments of leisure and in the hour of play, the knowledge that was acquired through much toil and effort. Hence it is that knowledge gained through logical methods becomes food for all the faculties of the mind, affording them exercise and recreation, the free indulgence in which induces culture. It is evident, therefore, that without the development of the intellectual faculties in their natural order and in harmonious proportion, the attainment of that higher and more complete culture involving the full growth of all the faculties of the mind, which gives power and efficiency, cannot be attained.

THE IMPORTANCE OF METHODICAL DEVELOPMENT OF THE INTELLECT.

The intellect must be developed methodically and the faculties must grow harmoniously. This development and this growth can be attained only by the proper exercise in their natural order of the knowing faculties of the mind. Antecedent to all methodical education there must be a thirst for knowledge, a desire to know. There must be a mental appetite to be gratified before mental food can be administered with profit. Precisely as the physical system is cloyed and injured by administering food when it is not wanted—that is, when there is no appetite demanding it—so all efforts at cramming the mind with mental pabulum will result in injury. The mind is in no sense a passive receptacle, a mere storehouse, in which may be lodged property and rubbish as the whim or the opportunity of the doorkeeper may permit, neither is it a blank tablet upon which any reckless scribbler may erasibly write. It is in itself an activity, a power, a being with susceptibilities; what it receives it has the power to retain or to reject, to store away for use or to cast forth as worthless. Its capacities are increased by the exercise arising from active use, or they are contracted by habits of idleness. A desire to know is the appetite for mental food, and as the body puts forth efforts to obtain aliment for its own life, so the mind, impelled by the sense of hunger and thirst for knowledge, goes out in search of it, and everywhere nature displays rich fields laden with abundant harvests, inviting all the activities of the mind to go forth, reap, garner and enjoy.

A system of education should have for its object the guidance of the faculties of the mind in their efforts to reap in the harvest-fields of nature, so that they may first gather that which is first required, that they may store away that which is of most use, to the end that the mind may be strengthened by labor, that the act of receiving may increase the capacity to receive, and that what requires greater strength and longer continued efforts to overcome and possess, may be left to be gathered at that period of life, when the requisite strength and power of endurance shall have been gained, through a judicious system of exercise.

A child employs its sense of hearing before its

sense of seeing, and both of these senses are used before it acquires the art of articulate speech; it uses its hands and arms in playing with its toys before it can use its feet and legs to walk for them. It would be extreme folly to insist that an infant shall not play with its rattle until it is able to walk to the table and get it, or that it should not be allowed the light of day, or to be guided by the sense of hearing, until the organs of speech are developed. It is equally illogical to attempt to cultivate the Reason and Understanding at that period when only the Senses are active, or to persist in efforts to store the Memory with abstractions, which cannot be understood, and to refuse to give exercise to the Senses in acquiring knowledge by observation until it can be acquired equally well through the operation of Reason. The system of education herewith presented is constructed upon this theory. It is a natural system because it provides for the development of the faculties in their natural order.

CONDITIONS FOR THE PROCESS OF EDUCATING.

Teaching presupposes three conditions: first, a degree of knowledge and capacity on the part of the pupil; second, a degree of knowledge and skill on the part of the teacher; and third, knowledge to be acquired. When a child enters school—and that is the period at which the system of education which is now under contemplation is designed to take effect—he possesses a certain amount of knowledge which has usually been acquired in an irregular way and is rarely systematically arranged as parts of theories or sciences, yet this knowledge is of great use to the pupil, and must be taken account of in efforts to lead the mind into regular habits of educating itself.

NATURAL PROCESS TO BE ENCOURAGED.

The knowledge possessed by the pupil has been acquired by observation; the first effort of the teacher, therefore, should be to encourage and systematize observation. This will bring order to the perceptions, will utilize the stores of the Memory and will exercise that faculty. It will bring order and strength to Recollection; it will utilize Imagination and will exercise Judgment. The nature of the mind and its natural order of development make it necessary that, in a system of education, the study of the material sciences should come first. It is entirely natural that a child should recognize differences between a rose and a geranium, between quartz and mica, before it can distinguish between *A* and *V* or *O* and *Q*. It is not too much to say, therefore, that for the young pupils, mere children, who are now forced to worry and wonder over what are to them meaningless characters, or who are required to sit in idleness under what seems to them a bitter and unnecessary restraint, a much more profitable use would be made of school-hours if they were taught to exercise their powers of observation and memory on the natural objects that surround them. Few farmers are able to name a tenth of the varieties of grasses, herbs and shrubs found in their fields, and an equal degree of ignorance prevails as to the names and qualities of rocks and soils. Under proper methods of instruction such knowledge would be acquired by pupils who enter school at the age of six, before the end of the second year of public-school education. In public schools established for the education of the people is a proper place to begin such a needed reform. Here is a practical work to undertake, here is popular ignorance to be dispelled, here are agreeable, profitable and easy lessons to be learned.

PUBLIC-SCHOOL EDUCATION.

Public schools are established for the instruction of the millions. The education provided in these schools should be practical, the methods should be agreeable and logical, and the results, popular intelligence. The reverse of this is mainly true; the education is almost universally impractical, the methods are disagreeable and illogical, and the result, purchased at the price paid for intelligence, is popular ignorance. Ten or fifteen years of school-life are given over to the study of illogical books, the solution of intricate problems found in school arithmetics, to the mastering of impractical methods and bungling devices, to the memorizing of useless and meaningless rules in grammar, correcting false syntax and parsing, to learning the names of places noted for the number of shoes made there or the quantity of cheese produced annually. This, coupled with the ability to read indifferently and write illegibly, in many places is all that is acquired by the majority of pupils in the public schools. This comparative uselessness of public-school education arises, not from want of intelligence on the part of the teacher, the convenience of appliances, skill in teaching or diligence in prosecuting studies, but in the most senseless and bungling methods of classification that are employed in the construction of the curriculum of studies. The facts of geology are more simple, more instructive and more useful than the facts of geography. The facts of anatomy, physiology and hygiene are more easily grasped than the facts of grammar and arithmetic, and with the exception of the fundamental rules, arithmetic should take its place behind geography, history and botany. The utterly extravagant value attached to mathematics as a means of disciplining the mind has led to incalculable mischief in times past, and has given to the world a generation of men absolutely ignorant of the plainest and most useful facts of science. This false estimate of the utility of one branch of learning over every other is felt from the lowest primary schools through all grades up to the universities. In the higher institutions mathematics is harnessed with the classics, making a double team which annually delivers for graduation hundreds of young men whose hearts are full of vanity and whose heads are full of ignorance. These are the "educated men" who give to society the numerous deplorable failures that long since brought "education" into disrepute. These men, graduating from the best colleges, ignorant of political history and of geography, ignorant of natural history, ignorant of every modern language, unfortunately ignorant of all useful learning except what is useful only for discipline, and, worse than all, "deplorably ignorant of their own ignorance,"—these "educated men," until within a very few years past, failing in every other pursuit in life, were teachers in public schools. They compressed the schools into their own narrowness, engrafted upon them their own barren methods, and made them failures like unto themselves—failures in this, that they consumed the school-years of the youth in forcing upon them instruction that is disagreeable and useless, and in withholding from them knowledge that would have been attractive, useful and ennobling.

"Mental arithmetic" and "higher arithmetic" should be excluded from the public schools. They are not sciences in any sense, but mere inventions brought forth by over-zealous mathematicians. Grammar might with some degree of profit, perhaps, be introduced into the schools during the last years of the course, but it is exceedingly doubtful whether any one in youth ever acquired, through grammar books, the ability to "speak and write the English language with propriety." Grammar in its true sense is a science of Language, but a science more intricate in its processes, more complex in its theories and more difficult to comprehend, than either of the physical sciences of which the facts lie at our feet on every side, which stretch out above and beneath us. Nevertheless, grammar is forced upon the pupil at a most tender age in most absurd methods, and it is held there year after year to the total exclusion of the more simple, useful and agreeable sciences, such as botany, geology, geography, chemistry, natural philosophy and astronomy.

The complicated inventions of men are studied first, while the simple and sublime creations of God are rarely studied at all in the public schools. The children are forced to feed on husks with swine, whilst the savory meats in the Father's house that strengthen and inspire are withheld. Stones and scorpions are given to the children who cry for bread and fish. In the system of education and the methods of teaching set forth in this work the old system, so barren of good results, so fruitful in failures, is rejected, and an artificial process is supplanted by a natural and logical order. Those subjects of study which are most simple, interesting and useful are introduced first. The more difficult and unnecessary—as grammar and mathematics—may follow as time and circumstances may permit them to be taken up. In the plan for organizing and conducting schools as here presented, it is the purpose of the author to lead teachers, school-directors and the parents of children educated in public schools into more pleasant and practical methods of labor. This will require no additional outlay of capital, will not involve an expenditure of more time, but will rather impart a degree of pleasure and profit to school-days hitherto not experienced by those who have preceded us as pupils and teachers.

PROFESSIONAL TRAINING FOR TEACHERS.

Against a continuation of a pernicious system of teaching the people at length protested. They demanded that normal schools should be established for the education of men and women in the "Art of Teaching." These institutions, now recognized in all parts of the country, are annually sending forth persons well qualified to teach, and as the number of these professional teachers increases, the system of teaching will become more logical, the education will be more effectual both in the quality of knowledge furnished and in the character of the men and women who shall be reared under its influence. Originally preceding, but now supplementing, the work of the normal schools, are "Teachers' Institutes" in counties and districts. These are gatherings of the teachers of a county or neighborhood at some convenient place for general instruction. In these Institutes methods of instruction are examined and criticised; there is an interchange of views on the subject of school government, and in this way teachers learn from each other what may be of practical use to them in their labors.

In States where normal schools have not yet

been established, teachers should combine for the purpose of holding Institutes during the vacation period. Expert teachers from other States may be employed, in addition to the best home talent, to instruct the teachers in the art of teaching. In these convocations the teachers are organized into classes in the several branches taught in the schools represented in the Institutes, and thus in class drills they learn by actual experience not only new truths, but also how to impart the knowledge of them to others.

The business of school teaching will be established as one of the learned professions only by enforcing a system of professional teaching, and with those educated in the art of teaching rests the responsibility of dignifying their vocation by the adoption of methods and processes, worthy of the high claims of professional dignity.

CHAPTER II.

DISCIPLINE.

GOVERNING FORCES.

THE passions and appetites of the animal stand lowest among all the forces in the human organism. These go out in innumerable cravings, in longings for gratification. Judgment and Reason take cognizance of these cravings of the flesh, contemplating them with reference to the results if they are unrestrained. Prudential considerations here have weight; the effect upon the body, the effect upon the social standing, the probability of concealment and other sordid considerations may determine the Judgment and Reason in arriving at a conclusion. This conclusion must, however, be carried up to the judgment-seat of Conscience. Here the sole question to be determined is one of absolute right. No other considerations can enter into the deliberations of this tribunal. Here the standard of absolute right is set up, and whatever is brought into this court is laid upon it, and if it is in harmony in every part and particular with this standard, it is approved, but not otherwise. After Conscience shall have pronounced the thing brought before it to be right or wrong, it is passed up to the Will-power, which is the human executive, for enforcement. Where the Will-power is weak, there is anarchy among the members, there is hesitation, there is indecision, there is feebleness, there is uncertainty of thought, doubtfulness in conclusion and inefficiency in action. If the Will-power is strong, the judgments of Conscience will be promptly and rigidly enforced. Harmony among all the departments or faculties of the mind will secure harmony of action. There will be wisdom to devise, righteousness to discriminate and power to enforce, and thus the animal passions will be kept in due subjection. The man whose mind is thus disciplined, being able to rule his own spirit, is "greater than he that taketh a city." A system of education must be so framed as to secure to the pupils, studying under its provisions, such harmonious and logical development as will afford data for the guidance of Judgment and Reason in the contemplation of the everyday life problems, that will be called up for legislative action; it must give such clearness and certainty of light to the human Conscience, as will enable it to discern the right from the wrong; it must give such power to the Will, as will enable it to execute with precision and promptness the judgments of Conscience. There must be discipline for the body and discipline for the mind. There must be intellectual culture and there must be moral culture, and all of these should be so directed and applied as to lead the pupil up to the higher, to the brighter and to the purer atmosphere of religious culture. In this necessity is found the occasion for a more extended and minute contemplation of the works of Nature, than has hitherto been thought expedient. The study of mathematics will give precision and definiteness to thought, the study of language and literature will give that social culture and suavity of manner that passes in the world for the refinement of education, but the study of the material sciences and the contemplation of the laws by which all things are governed leads directly from Nature up to Nature's God. The comprehension of the attributes of the Great Original is the end of all knowledge, and the most direct road thither is from the facts of creation, displayed to our senses, upward through the laws that bind them together. These are the works of the great Creator, and from the contemplation of his works it is easy and natural to rise to the contemplation of Him who made and ruleth over all.

What is here written is for the guidance of those, who are immediately concerned in common-school education. The idea is not to discard mathematics, language and literature as educational forces, but to insist that their place is logically and naturally after instead of before the material sciences. The children in the public schools must not be compelled to waste their school-days in the study of mathematics, grammar and literature, to the exclusion of the more agreeable and more profitable studies in the field of Nature. In the chapter on higher education the scope and uses of mathematics and the classics as means of education will be again considered. The object here is to show, that for purposes of discipline to the young mind, the facts of the material sciences are in every sense superior to those of mathematics and language.

THE USES OF DISCIPLINE.

The value of discipline consists chiefly in this, that it creates a desire for the acquisition of knowledge and directs the efforts by logical methods, which, from the beginning, contemplate an attainable end. To those, therefore who labor among the material elements of nature, such as the soil, the plants, the rocks, the waters, the winds and the animals, that learning which will best enable them to observe the characteristics of the things among which they toil will be to them most valuable. It will give them both skill to observe and wisdom to apply. Either for the uses of art or for the advancement of science, such an education is much more reasonable than that which gives the power to solve intricate problems in mathematics, or to analyze and parse obscurely-constructed passages in English literature.

THEORY WITHOUT PRACTICE.

Many fierce battles of controversy have been fought. Conservatives, on the one side, have bitterly contended for what is old and well tried. Enthusiastic reformers, on the other side, have insisted upon a total overthrow of the college curriculum, the rejection of ancient languages and literature from the new catalogue of studies and the substitution of the technical sciences in their stead. Though singular, it is not inexplicable, that both of these contending forces are in error. The conservatives, appealing to the universal experience of educators, seem to forget "that a teacher's experience must be measured, not by the length of time that he has been engaged in his work, but rather by the amount of analytical ability and intellectual labor that he has applied to the materials which that experience has furnished him." Opportunities for observation and experiment may be great, but the faculty of evolving truth and of forming logical conclusions may be small. Most of the successful instructors in the higher institutions of learning have derived their theories of education by intuition from the college atmosphere, and these remain undigested and unchanged, their personal experience having wrought no modification in what was dogmatically laid upon them by their predecessors. It frequently happens, therefore, that the continuance of the old curriculum is insisted upon simply because neither observation nor experience has suggested to the minds of those persistent conservatives the necessity for any departure from it. On the other hand, those who insist upon so radical a change as the exclusion of the classics from the college course are so hedged in with the idea of utility, that they reject everything that is not in accordance with their own notion of immediate practical use. Thus it happens that "the history of education is both the battle-field and burying-ground of impracticable theories." *

* Sidgwick.

NATURAL AND ARTIFICIAL SYSTEMS.

All methods of education may be reduced to two general systems, the natural and the artificial. By natural education is meant that which teaches pupils those things in which they are likely to be interested in after-life. It is not proposed that education should always be technical, but in that preliminary training which precedes professional preparation respect should be had to the probable condition of the pupil through life, and his education should be shaped with reference to that condition, and yet with a view to giving as liberal a culture as is compatible with the extent of the school period he is likely to enjoy.

An artificial education is one in which pupils are taught one thing that they may ultimately know another. "It teaches a boy the rudiments of some learning or accomplishments that a man will be content to forget," but by this process of learning in order to forget he is prepared to grapple with the practical problems of life with some certainty of mastering them. It is claimed by the advocates of the artificial system, that it is the only safe course to ensure that discipline and culture, which everywhere distinguishes the educated gentleman from the mere superficial pretender. They assume that this training and discipline is unattainable through any method whereby useful knowledge is directly acquired. Herein consists their fundamental error. It is now admitted by many of the ablest schoolmen and the wisest philosophers, that the teaching of useful knowledge affords as valuable a training to the mind as it is possible to attain by any system of instruction.

Study for the purposes of discipline only is study from pure love for learning. This indeed is a noble impulse that should be encouraged wherever it is found, but a system of education, that puts forward such learning as that best adapted to the millions of people, who compose the population of any country, is radically defective. In a curriculum for general education, framed for the use of the people, those branches of learning that are studied from pure curiosity or from the love of research are precisely those that should be excluded. They may with propriety find a place in those higher institutions of learning, wherein are found young men and women with means and leisure at their command to pursue literary and scientific investigation for the good of mankind, or as a source of gratification to themselves. Literary and private institutions may very properly adopt the artificial method of education, but those who construct a system of public schools for the training of the youth of all classes, and especially of the active productive laboring classes, must hold to the natural system.

THE SCOPE OF PUBLIC-SCHOOL EDUCATION.

It will not be denied by men who carefully survey the field, that common-school education is intended more as a universal system, contrived to supply, at a small cost, useful information to the masses. It is not intended to provide for that liberal culture which only a few are ambitious to attain and still fewer succeed in acquiring. The chief aim, therefore, should be the development of the faculties of external observation. It is not enough that pupils learn merely to see things as they are. The memory must be taught to record accurately, and the imagination to represent faithfully, the facts observed. The materials on which the intellect ordinarily acts, even when thinking apart from observing, are ideas of the external world. There is food in the elements of the material sciences both for the imaginative and conceptive faculties, and the training which is furnished in the act of classifying the things observed, is precisely the education that will be useful in the business of life. The student is required not merely to apply the classification made to order, but he is frequently required to construct a classification for immediate use. Neither the study of mathematics nor of literature cultivates habits of reasoning from effects to causes and from causes to effects.

Life is a series of unfinished systems. At every period something is present and something is absent. This is precisely the case in physics. The study of them, therefore, is the most natural and efficacious way of teaching how to correctly infer and combine absent phenomena with present phenomena in the perceptions. In reference to the study of physical science, Cuvier very justly observes, "Every transaction which supposes a classification of facts, every research which requires a distribution of matter, is performed after the same manner, and he who has cultivated this science merely for amusement is surprised at the facilities it affords for disentangling all kinds of affairs." A system of education should afford proper discipline to the mind and at the same time stimulate it to active exercise, and in this respect the study of the sciences has the advantage over all other branches of learning for young pupils. The books which they open to the student will never be shut up and put away. The external world, directly and indirectly, daily forces itself upon the observation, and it will be of continual advantage to be able to comprehend and classify the observations thus passing before us. The superiority of the material sciences as subjects for school studies is also felt in this: they teach the pupil what in all periods of life he is most glad to know.

THE IMPORTANCE OF THE PHYSICAL SCIENCES.

An eminent scholar of England who very forcibly reviews the relative value of studies says: "Physical science is now so bound up with all the interests of mankind, from the lowest and most material to the loftiest and most profound, it is so engrossing in its infinite detail, so exciting in its progress and promise, so fascinating in the varied beauty of its revelations,—that it draws to itself an ever-increasing amount of intellectual energy, so that the intellectual man who has been trained without it must feel at every turn his inability to comprehend thoroughly the present phase of the progress of humanity, and his limited sympathy with the thoughts and feelings, labors and aspirations, of his fellow-men. And if there be any who believe that the summit of a liberal education, the crown of the highest culture, is philosophy—meaning by philosophy the sustained effort, if it be no more than an effort, to frame a complete and reasoned synthesis of the facts of the universe—on them it may be especially urged how poorly equipped a man comes to such a study, however competent he may be to interpret the thoughts of ancient thinkers, if he has not qualified himself to examine, comprehensively and closely, the wonderful scale of methods by which the human mind has achieved its various degrees of conquest over the world of Sense."

Noah Porter, President of Yale College, says: "Botany and mineralogy, with the elements of geology, especially botany, are branches which can be acquired in early life, which is the observing period, provided an exciting interest can be aroused in their objects. We cannot estimate too highly the habits which are induced by these studies, or the tastes which they awaken and refine. The nice eye for analysis, the attentive eye for research, the enterprise and self-reliance required for open-air excursions, the elevating influences that come from a contact with the purity and beauty of nature, and the habits of ready tact and rapid induction which such studies and researches involve,—are all invaluable features of the character, and leave priceless treasures for life. No one can appreciate more highly than we the tastes and aptitudes of the enthusiastic naturalist, whether seen in their blossom in the youthful votary or in their ripeness in the matured philosopher. We would therefore insist that those sciences should be studied thoroughly in the preparatory education, so far as they are mainly sciences of observation and of fact."

Discoursing upon the practical uses of study, the same high authority says, "The pure mathematics, both elementary and advanced, are the least directly practical of any sciences, and it is only because of their necessity as the foundation of the applied sciences and arts that they are so readily admitted into the circle of practical and useful knowledge."

For purposes of discipline, therefore, within the sphere of public-school education, the conclusion that the study of the material sciences stands pre-éminent will not be seriously controverted.

CHAPTER III.

SCHOOL AUTHORITIES.

IN each of the States there is a school department possessing some form of organization, charged with the performance of specific duties and limited to the exercise of definite powers. This department usually is charged with a general supervision over the educational affairs of the State. It collects statistics, publishes reports, and in a general way is a means of communication between the Legislature and the people.

LOCAL AUTHORITIES.

Every State is subdivided into school districts of greater or less dimensions; within these districts are local authorities, which may be designated by the general name of "School Boards." To these local authorities is intrusted by the people the business of establishing, supporting and conducting schools. This involves the raising of revenues, the erecting of school-buildings, the fixing of the school-term, its duration and time for opening and closing, the construction of a course of study, the fixing the amount of salary to be paid, the employment of teachers, the care of school property, the inspection of the schools, and generally the doing of whatever is necessary for the establishing and maintaining of schools for the proper education of the children within their jurisdiction. These local officers are usually elected by the people, and are therefore immediately accountable to them for the faithful discharge of their duties. In most States the manner in which money shall be raised for the support of schools, as well as the minimum length of the school term, is fixed by law.

DUTIES OF LOCAL AUTHORITIES.

The duties of the local authorities will be treated under the following general subdivisions —first, as applicable to rural districts:

1st. Schoolhouses—buildings, furniture and grounds.

2d. School-term.

3d. Course of study.

4th. The adoption of books.

5th. Salary of teachers.

6th. Employment of teachers.

7th. Supervision.

SCHOOLHOUSES.

The first duty of the local authorities in every district is to see that every neighborhood is provided with a convenient schoolhouse. It too frequently happens that a site for a schoolhouse is chosen solely with reference to its cheapness. In rural districts a building is erected by the roadside in a low, wet, unshaded spot, frequently upon a piece of ground that is utterly useless for any other purpose, and ought also to be considered wholly unfit for the purpose to which it is applied. In the first place, the site should be central in the neighborhood which it is intended to accommodate, it should be easily accessible, and it should be on elevated and well-drained grounds. After an eligible site has been selected, sufficient ground should be purchased to admit of a convenient playground extending on every side of the building. If this can be found in a grove of old trees, it will be the more desirable.

The building should be erected upon an improved plan of school architecture, and with sole reference to the uses to which it is to be put. A house for the accommodation of a mixed school in a rural district should be provided with a spacious vestibule and separate dressing-rooms for the girls and boys, with closets in which to store away the dinner-baskets, and hooks upon which to hang the outer garments worn by the children. The building should be sufficiently elevated from the ground to ensure dryness, and should be provided with the most approved contrivances for ventilating; the heating apparatus should be constructed with reference to efficiency both in warming and ventilating the study-rooms.

FURNITURE.

The furniture of the schoolhouse should be of the most approved and convenient pattern. The desks should be so arranged as to enable all pupils to pass to and from their seats without disturbing each other and without creating confusion in any part of the room.

Every school should be provided with a library of reference-books. These should be the property of the district, and be accessible to all the pupils. The most comprehensive English dictionary, a geographical gazetteer, a biographical dictionary, a popular encyclopædia, sets of historical and physiological charts and outline maps should be considered indispensable articles in the furnishing of every school-house.

The teacher's desk should be so constructed as to be well adapted to the uses for which it is intended. A plain business office desk, with drawers, shelves, closets and book-rack, is perhaps the most convenient form. School-officers should not set their teachers down to tables without drawer, shelf or lock, and expect them to keep accurate records of the transactions in school. All the movable property in and about the schoolroom should be intrusted to the care of the treasurer of the school-board, who should be held responsible for its safe-keeping.

THE GROUNDS.

The grounds about a schoolhouse should be thoroughly drained, so as to ensure dryness in all seasons. They should be leveled and sodded, and, if not already supplied, should be planted with trees for shade and with hardy shrubs for ornament. A house for fuel and separate closets for the accommodation of the pupils of both sexes should be provided, and the teacher should be instructed to see that these are always kept clean. Upon the grounds of every schoolhouse there should be a supply of water. This will add to the cleanliness and to the health of all who may attend the school. And, finally, a neat fence should enclose the whole, and this by annual repair and frequent painting should be maintained in good condition. A shabby schoolhouse is a disgrace to any neighborhood.

CITY SCHOOLHOUSES.

The directions given above with reference to schoolhouses, school-furniture and school-grounds are intended for rural districts. In cities and large towns, where schools are graded, there is opportunity for the erection of school-buildings that for convenience and ornament would not be excelled by the architectural achievements in any other department of public or private enterprise. Near the centre of the school-district in cities a lot of suitable size should be obtained, and a master-architect should be employed to design a building after the best models of school-architecture. Sole reference should be had to the number of classes that are to be taught in the school, the number of teachers that are to be employed and the extent of the course of studies that is to be pursued. A community can rarely find a place where the expenditure of money for public uses can be more profitably made than in providing first-class school-buildings. The very first requisite is an abundance of space; the next, convenience of arrangement, and, perhaps more important than all, the certainty of strength in every part of the building, with ample facilities of ingress and egress to every department. In some of the large cities the school authorities, for some inexplicable reason, have erected their school-buildings on narrow streets or on filthy alleys. There can be no stronger evidence of the lack of wisdom on the part of these authorities than the selection of such improper places as sites for schoolhouses. In other cities lots facing open squares and the widest and most airy streets are selected for school purposes, and this is evidence of a proper appreciation on the part of the local authorities of what is best for the community. A city high school should be supplied with all of the most approved apparatus that can be of use to illustrate and enforce the facts and principles of the branches taught in the school. The furniture should be of the most approved kind, and everything within and about the school-building, the furniture and the apartments should be surrounded with an air of neatness and order that will at once attract attention and engender agreeable emotions.

SCHOOL-TERM.

The length of the school-term, wherever it is fixed by law, is usually adapted to the average ability of the several districts in the State to incur the expenses of supporting schools. The right to extend the term beyond the minimum fixed by law is usually left to the local school authorities. Schools should be kept open everywhere during at least six months in the year, and wherever it is practicable the term should be extended to nine months. In rural districts, during the season of inclement weather, it is unsafe for the younger pupils to go any distance to school, and during the busy season of the summer months the larger boys cannot conveniently be spared from the labors of the farm or the workshop. Where the school is opened at the beginning of the month of September and closed in March or April, the younger children will be the first to present themselves for instruction. During the winter months their places will be occupied by their older brothers and sisters. This will especially be the case in rural districts in northern latitudes. Though the disarrangement of classes that will arise may not be agreeable to the teacher, it is less objectionable than to have two short terms, one in the winter and one in the summer.

Inasmuch as the common-school education is the only education obtained by a very large proportion of all the children in the United States, it is of the utmost importance that the school authorities provide for the longest annual term that the financial condition of the district will admit of. As the people of a State become more prosperous and wealthy, the Legislature should increase the minimum length of the school-term, so as to encourage the inhabitants of all parts of the State in educational progress.

COURSE OF STUDY.

The course of studies pursued in each school should not be left to the whim of the pupils or to the option of the teacher. Everywhere the school authorities should determine what branches of learning shall be taught in the schools within their jurisdiction. The men, who are chosen by the people to conduct educational affairs in the district, are usually the most competent judges of what sort of knowledge will be of most use to the children that will attend the schools. Many branches are common, and should be taught everywhere. Others are more technical, and are peculiarly adapted to the uses of people engaged in special pursuits. For purposes of discipline, the general principles of mineralogy and mining engineering, the principles of mechanics and manufacturing engineering, are equal, whereas, for practical utility, the former would be eminently proper in a mining region, and the latter in a manufacturing community. So with regard to the principles of navigation and agriculture. The former would be proper in schools for the education of the children of a seaboard community, and the latter for the agricultural districts throughout the land.

Text-books on all of these and kindred subjects have been prepared, and the school authorities should make provision for instruction in those special branches that are adapted to the wants of the community.

As common-school education is necessarily limited in its extent, it is important that the time of the pupil and the effort of the teacher be not expended in endeavoring to exhaust two or three branches of learning; the course of study should be so arranged as to afford practical instruction in the primary elements of as many branches of learning as can be successfully taught in the time and with the appliances common to our public schools. Thus, instead of attempting to make expert mathematicians of all the boys and girls, who attend public schools, by cramming them with "mental arithmetic," "common-school arithmetic," "higher arithmetic" and "university arithmetic," it would be vastly more useful, whether considered with reference to discipline or the acquisition of knowledge or for purposes of culture, to lay aside the subject of mathematics at the end of the common-school arithmetic, and to give the additional time, which is now generally wasted on the so-called higher books, to the study of botany, physiology, natural philosophy and other sciences. So also with reference to grammar.

Instead of attempting to make critical grammarians, magazine writers or poets of the boys and girls, it would serve a much better purpose to give the whole time, that is now usually misapplied in the study of grammar, to the study of history, chemistry and geology.

Be it understood all teaching must be thorough, but thoroughness and quantity are in no sense synonymous terms. A thorough knowledge of the fundamental rules of arithmetic is acquired at a very early period of school-life. It is the bungling, useless, impractical devices constituting the bulk of the matter found in the mental and higher arithmetics that consume the time of the pupil. More knowledge, more discipline and higher culture are found in the pursuit of other studies, and therefore the importance of taking these up. A little knowledge is not a dangerous thing. The smallest modicum of knowledge is useful to the possessor of it. It is the superficial effort at learning a great deal, but which leaves in the mind a definite knowledge of nothing, that is popularly called a "little learning," and this it is that is dangerous.

A thorough mastering of any branch of learning requires years of toil and maturity of mind. Neither of these comports with the scope of the public schools. The years of the pupil and the nature of the situation admit only of the teaching of the elements. It will be far more conducive to popular education to introduce more branches, the elements of which may be comprehended by young pupils, than to attempt to pursue to a greater extent only a few of the subjects now most popular with teachers. The boards of education in city and country should, therefore, so arrange the course of study for the schools under their supervision, as to increase the number of subjects by shortening the time devoted to each.

ADOPTION OF BOOKS.

The local school authorities should adopt a series of books to be used in the schools of their district. In order to do this intelligently certain preliminary questions must be settled: 1st. It must be determined what branches of learning shall be taught in the several schools; 2d. To what extent these shall be taught; and 3d. The number of reference-books to be supplied to each school. Reading, writing, arithmetic, geography, grammar, composition and declamation are taught in all, or nearly all, of the schools in city and country. To these should be added history, physiology, botany, natural philosophy, chemistry and geology. As elsewhere stated, it will be necessary to restrict the teaching of arithmetic, geography and grammar within reasonable common-school limits, in order to make room for the teaching of the material sciences. If this restraint is not imposed by the local school authorities, the pupils of the schools in the district will be defrauded of much of the most agreeable and useful knowledge naturally within the scope of public-school education. To enforce such limitations the school-boards should adopt but one book on arithmetic. This should be selected with reference to its suitability for the teaching and study of the fundamental rules, and beyond this teachers of mixed schools should not be allowed to carry their classes. The admission of books of mental arithmetic and higher arithmetic will open wide the door for the increase of those innumerable absurdities and devices, hitherto tolerated on the plea of discipline, but now excluded for more useful branches of learning.

A geography for public-school purposes must also be comprised within the limits of one convenient book. Primary, secondary and comprehensive geographies must be rejected, and the work of some author who, with a proper appreciation of the wants of the schools, has been able to compress the essential parts of the subject within proper limits for these schools, should be adopted.

Grammar, far beyond what it is profitable for

the pupils in the public schools to study, can be set forth in one small volume. Such a book should be found and adopted.

There must also be a limit fixed for the number of Readers to be used in the public schools. Many ingeniously constructed arguments have been devised for the purpose of proving the utility of a series of many books, but no good reason can be given why the number of Readers should exceed three, the first beginning with the alphabet and the third ending with such exercises in reading as will be adapted to the wants of the most advanced classes in ungraded schools. For purposes of declamation, which in this country, where almost every man has occasion to give public expression to his views on many subjects, is a very important branch of study, and one which should find a place in every school, a "speaker" or book of selections should be added to the series of Readers.

A system of penmanship and of vocal music added to the foregoing will constitute what has hitherto been regarded a sufficient course of study for the public schools. It is now proposed, however, to occupy the time which has been saved by abridging the study of arithmetic, geography and grammar in the study of physiology, botany, natural philosophy, chemistry and geology. Suitable text-books on all of these sciences have been prepared especially for the use of schools. There is little danger that school-boards will introduce too many branches of learning, but there is great danger that they will admit too many books and permit the consumption of too much time on special subjects.

After a series of books, covering all the subjects intended to be taught in the school, shall have been selected, let the action of the board be as the laws of the Medes and Persians—irrevocable. There is no part of the administration of the public-school system in which there is greater demand for unwavering firmness, than in the adoption and maintenance of a series of books for each district. Publishers and publishers' agents will, by specious arguments, corruption, bribery and fraud, labor in season and out of season to persuade school-boards, that the books in use in their schools are inferior, and that the books offered at "adoption rates," "absurdly cheap," are in every respect superior. Generally, these arguments, if they may be thus dignified, are the merest fictions; by listening to them incalculable mischief may result to the people's schools. In a score of Readers, an equal number of Arithmetics, Geographies and Grammars by as many authors, there cannot be found a sufficient difference of merit to warrant a change from one to the other, even if the proposed new books were to be supplied gratuitously during a year. The duty of local school-boards in this matter can be summed up in two brief formulas: first, adopt a good series of books, and, secondly, refuse to make any changes until time and the progress of science shall make apparent the necessity for change. The frequent change of text-books embarrasses the teacher, confuses the pupils and wastes the money of the people. It is a loss without recompense to all, excepting only booksellers and bookmakers.

SALARY.

The question of salary is very properly left to the local authorities for adjustment. In different localities different prices are paid for labor. The same laws that govern prices in other professions and vocations should obtain in paying teachers. Generally, the salaries paid for this important service are much below the sums that like ability commands in almost any other position. In many of the large cities, where bricklayers and carpenters command from three dollars to five dollars per day, and where clerks and bookkeepers of ordinary capacity receive from fifteen hundred dollars to two thousand dollars per annum, school-teachers who receive one thousand dollars a year are thought to be exceedingly well paid; in many places where house-servants receive from two dollars and a half to three dollars a week, with boarding and the comforts of home, a lady teaching school and receiving three hundred dollars a year for her work, and paying half of it for boarding, is regarded as highly favored in the way of emoluments. The fact that more money is commanded by a like amount of talent and skill in almost any other vocation is the chief cause of the want of experienced teachers, everywhere so keenly felt. The districts, therefore, that are able to pay fair salaries for fair qualifications, and thus secure the services during a number of years of a corps of well-qualified teachers, are exceedingly fortunate. If the inhabitants in any district would combine and provide dwelling-houses for their teachers, and thus settle them permanently, paying them reasonable compensation, they would derive incalculable benefits therefrom. No time need then be lost, year after year, in teachers and pupils learning to know each other, and in the teacher ascertaining the capacity of his pupils and the wants of the district, and this would well repay the taxpayers for such investment. Statistics in some of the Eastern States show, that more than eighty per cent. of the teachers employed in the public schools serve in that capacity during a period of less than one year. Or, to reverse the statement, only about twenty per centum of the teaching force of the United States brings to the labors of the school-room any professional experience. It need not be argued that this in itself is one of the most serious obstructions to public-school progress. Whatever, therefore, can be done to increase the number of experienced teachers, will greatly benefit those who attend the schools. One of the most powerful influences operating to draw active, intelligent and well-educated young men and young women from school-room work is the fact, that their time and talents command higher wages in other spheres of labor. The local authorities, therefore, should regard it as the very worst economy to attempt to save money by keeping down the salaries paid to teachers. It may with much more profit be saved on buildings, grounds, furniture and books, but with infinitely more profit on many other things in no way connected with public-school education.

No specific directions can be given on this subject. The financial condition of the district, the appreciation of the people for learning and their willingness to have their children educated in the public schools will determine the question. The utmost effort should be put forth to advance the price paid for teaching, and the salaries should be graded according to qualification, and not according to age or sex. Women who do the work as thoroughly are entitled to the same pay that men would receive in the same position. Generally, it will be found that better talent and higher qualifications can be obtained for a given sum by employing ladies. They are more likely, also, to remain in the profession, for the reason that fewer places of labor are open to them.

EXAMINATION AND EMPLOYMENT OF TEACHERS.

Before a teacher is employed to take charge of a school, he should be examined in order to ascertain whether he possesses proper qualifications for the position he expects to occupy. In every examination of teachers two qualifications are to be discovered: 1st. The possession of the requisite knowledge; 2d. The possession of the requisite skill. A person may possess knowledge, and yet not have skill to communicate that knowledge to others. The examination, therefore, should be directed chiefly to ascertain whether the applicant possesses skill to impart knowledge. If he is an experienced teacher, he should be able to produce certificates of his skill from the school authorities under whose jurisdiction he had been employed.

If the examination is skillfully conducted, the answer to every question propounded by the examiner will show whether the examined has mastered the art of his profession. It is a lamentable fact that in a large majority of cases the examination is most illogically conducted. Teachers are made to puzzle their brains over the solutions of intricate problems in mathematics, or the explanation of disputed points in grammar, or the spelling of words not found in the literature of the times, nor used by any of the great writers in poetry or prose, or to give the boundaries of some out-of-the-way province or the locality of some obscure point on the earth's surface. The ability to answer such questions divulges the fact that the teacher is a mere curiosity-monger, and has employed his time in the finding out of unusual and useless things. He is, therefore, of all men the most unfit to teach a school. A much more sensible and useful method of examining teachers is to require each applicant, to exhibit to the examiner and to the school authorities present, in what manner he would explain the principles of arithmetic to a class, in what manner he would introduce the subject of botany, how he would explain to a class the astronomical principles involved in the study of geography, and how he would begin the study of grammar. The answer to such questions will at once discover whether the person answering them possesses knowledge accompanied with skill to instruct others.

School superintendents and persons usually employed to examine teachers follow too closely the method adopted by the colleges, forgetting, or seeming, indeed, never to have known, that the objects of the two examinations are wholly dissimilar. A college professor wishes simply to discover whether the applicant for matriculation possesses the amount of knowledge, on specific subjects, requisite to enter the classes he proposes to join; whereas the school authorities wish to know whether the applicant is skilled in the art of communicating knowledge to the untaught.

Higher Qualifications.—It is admitted by all schoolmen that he, who possesses a knowledge simply of the branches to be taught in a school, and that, too, only so far as the purposes of the school may require, is indeed a very superficial teacher. To every branch of learning there are many collaterals which explain the principles of and extend the knowledge on the subject. A teacher should be familiar with these collateral, or co-ordinate branches of learning. A formal examination, therefore, of an applicant for the position of teacher in the branches required to be taught in the district, will simply exhibit the teacher's ability to explain certain technical facts.

It shows no general comprehension of the subject, no thoroughness of knowledge, no general observation, no liberal culture; in short, this examination in no sense discovers whether or not an applicant possesses, that general discipline of mind and accumulation of knowledge, which would enable him to lift up the school from the mere routine work of study and recitation, as laid down in the books, to higher achievements. A general conversation between a teacher and an intelligent school-board will serve to draw out the teacher's powers.*

It is not intended to suggest that the tech-

* In one of the counties in Pennsylvania most advanced on the subject of education, the school-directors of a township containing thirteen schools had convened for the annual examination and employment of teachers. The forenoon was consumed in the transaction of general miscellaneous business. Dinner was provided at a village hotel. Upon one end of the table was a large roast of beef. Opposite to this, on one side of the table, was an old gentleman, a member of the school-board, and on the other side was a young man not yet arrived at the age of his majority, an applicant for a school in the district. The old gentleman took up the carving-knife and handed it across the table to the young man with a request that he should carve the roast. With perfect composure the young man took the knife and fork, carved the roast and served the gentlemen about the table. When the dinner was over, the school-officer took the young man aside, and after a conversation of ten minutes said to him, "I want you to come to our village and teach our school." The old gentleman had discovered in the manners of the young man at the table that which led him to believe that he had enjoyed a liberal training, and that he possessed those qualifications which would make him a successful teacher. Subsequent events fully justified this opinion, for the school under his charge became soon one of the most celebrated in the county, and though he remained but two years in the village, seventeen of his pupils became school-teachers.

nical examination is to be dispensed with, but rather that this examination shall not be over-estimated in its usefulness. The possession of a liberal culture and a wide range of information will be discovered much more readily, in a general conversation on each branch presented, than by any system of mere technical examination that can be devised.

Every examination of teachers should be conducted in the presence of the school authorities, and no member of the board of education should be, for light considerations, excused from being present, when the persons who are to be employed as teachers in the district are examined.

Professional Certificates.—It is essential to the elevation and dignity of the profession that provision be made for the granting of professional certificates, the holders of which should be everywhere exempt from the ordeal of a re-examination as now conducted, but they should not be exempt from such inspection as will exhibit to the authorities, by whom they are to be employed, the possession of such qualifications as they desire to secure for the use of the schools in their district. It will not be necessary, for this purpose alone, to secure the presence of an official examiner. An intelligent school-board will be able, by a direct conversation on the subject of school-teaching, the branches to be taught and the manner of teaching them, to ascertain whether the applicant for employment in their district possesses the requisite qualifications. This, whilst it is certainly more in keeping with professional dignity, is also more practical and reasonable when the fact is kept in view, that a professional certificate, generally, is evidence of knowledge possessed, and the only thing left for the board to discover is, whether the person holding the certificate is endowed with such general qualities and has attained that degree of culture, which will make him desirable as a teacher for their neighborhood.

SUPERVISION.

A proper supervision of the schools in any district is an important, and at the same time a very delicate, duty. Two general systems are in use. The oldest, and also the most unsatisfactory, is the committee system. The school-board divides itself into committees, the members of which by turns visit the schools. Under this system the supervision amounts to little more than occasional informal visits to the school-room, where a useless interruption of the school and a useless conversation with the teacher occur; the conversation is more frequently on the condition of the weather, the school furniture, the supply of fuel and other equally unprofessional and irrelevant topics, than upon the management of the school, the methods of teaching and the progress made. Occasionally it happens that some member of the school-board possesses the requisite qualifications, and has sufficient leisure to enable him to visit the schools with some degree of regularity. When this is the case, and such a member of the board can be induced to undertake the work, some good may result by such departure from the committee system.

There is, however, but one system by which efficient and satisfactory supervision can be obtained, and that is by the employment of a proper person as district, city or county superintendent. In many of the States provision is made by acts of Assembly for the employment of school superintendents. In some States one superintendent is employed for each Congressional district. In others one is employed for each county, and in others special districts are established for school purposes. In some of the States laws have been enacted providing for the appointment of city and district superintendents, who preside over smaller districts, and therefore render a more efficient service than it is possible to obtain from an officer who has charge of a larger division of the State.

In the manner of appointment, the scope of duties, the qualifications required and general utility, there is a wide difference in this office and officer in the several States. The system which has given most satisfaction to persons interested in the efficiency of public schools is that, in which the superintendent is chosen by local boards of directors or of education, as the case may be, in the district over which the superintendent is to preside. The choice of this officer is thus removed from the excitement and from the demoralizing influences of political campaigns. It makes him to a proper degree responsible to the local school authorities. It enables those who best know what is required to select a person of proper qualifications for the office. In some cases the directors also fix the compensation which the superintendent shall receive, and prescribe the duties that he shall perform. In some States the law prescribes that the superintendent shall not only be learned in the arts, sciences and literature, but that he shall be experienced in the art of teaching. A strong argument in favor of this system is, it gives harmony and unity to the school authorities within the district, it keeps the school management as far removed as possible from the corrupting influences of party politics, and, in the third place, it makes the superintendent dependent for continuance in office upon the people whom he serves. These advantages are likely to be lost to the people in those States where superintendents are chosen by ballot at general elections, or where they are appointed by some central State authority.

Whenever it shall occur that a county or district is so large that one superintendent cannot exercise a close and thorough supervision of the schools under his jurisdiction, the local school authorities should, by petition to the Legislature for power, or otherwise, procure a division of the district, or permission to appoint local superintendents, who might preside over sub-districts and report to the general superintendent. It has now become almost a universal practice among superintendents to conduct the examination of teachers in the presence of school-boards. This duty involves severe labor on the part of the superintendent.

Boards of education, everywhere, should provide for a thorough supervision, by the employment of a proper and well-cultivated person to perform that duty. The appointment of such an officer does not, however, release the members of school-boards from exercising a general supervision over the schools under their charge. They should require frequent reports from the superintendents, they should be present at all examinations, and they should visit as often as practicable, and the oftener the better, the schools for the good conduct of which they are responsible to the people.

Out of School.—Theoretically, the State provides for the education of every child within its borders. It is a notorious and lamentable reflection, that in every State in the Union many children never attend the public schools, or any other schools, or attend so irregularly or for so short a time as to derive very little benefit from them. The local school authorities should hold it to be one of their highest duties to insist upon a regular attendance, or as nearly so as practicable, from every child in the district. School-officers should make it their business to visit such families as neglect to send their children to school, and by persuasion, if possible, induce these short-sighted parents to give to their children the advantages of such an education as the public schools afford. There can be but little doubt, that half the delinquency in any district could be removed by judicious efforts put forth by the school-board in this direction. Part of the work of supervision, therefore, consists of placing in well-provided schools all of the eligible children in the Commonwealth, and until this is fully accomplished, the school authorities in the localities where children are out of school may be reasonably held to be derelict in the discharge of their duties. It is true, this may be regarded as extra-official work. It has hitherto been unrecognized as a duty, yet it is unquestionably one of the most important services that a school-officer can render to the Commonwealth. If schools are provided, convenient for all, and if all enjoy the advantages of these provisions, then the system obtains its full force, and the authorities, to whom the application of the system is intrusted, have discharged their full duties to the public who have placed with them a most sacred trust.

CHAPTER IV.

ORGANIZATION.

A TEACHER, who has been elected to take charge of a school in a neighborhood where he is a stranger, should without delay, cultivate the acquaintance of the families that reside in the district. There is but one way to accomplish this effectually, and that is by a personal visit made to each household. This may consume a week or more of the time just preceding the opening of the school, but there is no better use to which it can be put. Such visits will convince the people that the teacher takes an interest in his work and desires to do it well. He, therefore, in the beginning, secures the confidence of those most interested in the success of his school. He should not go from house to house armed with book and pencil, as a census-taker would go, but should call as one desiring to cultivate the acquaintance of the families, and after having modestly introduced himself, enter into a general conversation on the subject of the school; thus he may ascertain how many children from each family will be likely to attend school, what their ages and advancements are, and what books they have studied. From the children he can learn who were in the several classes, how many classes there were in the school, how the school was organized, and many other matters of detail that will assist him in making up a complete schedule of classes and studies, ready for use on the opening day. The facts gathered from house to house, that are of sufficient importance to be remembered, should be entered in a mem orandum-book convenient for reference. Not the least of the advantages arising from this practice will be an increased attendance on the first day of school. There will have been established beforehand an acquaintance between the teacher and his pupils, and that will facilitate their coming to an understanding on the organization of the work of the school.

With all the facts that may be gathered by visiting, as above suggested, before him, the teacher may construct a hypothetical organization. A time-table for exercises and a schedule of studies and a general plan may be mapped out. This will enable the teacher to construct his classes, and to begin work systematically from the opening of the school on the first day.

The chief business of the teacher on the first day is to win the respect of the pupils, and to establish confidence between them and himself. Nothing will go farther to accomplish this than a systematic beginning. The fact that the teacher has ascertained the names of all the children in the neighborhood, and has arranged them into classes, will enable him to classify all the pupils who present themselves at the opening of the school, to assign places for beginning each study, and to post a time-table in a convenient place in the school-room, that with slight variation will become the permanent order of exercises during the term. This of itself will not fail to please the pupils, and to give them full confidence in the teacher's ability to "keep" a good school.

ORDER OF EXERCISES.

In constructing an order of exercises, this general principle should be followed: the young classes and the simplest lessons should come first in the morning. These may be considered as constituting the first general division in the school. The second division would comprise the pupils who are engaged in the more advanced branches of study. When the lessons of the first division shall have been disposed of, those in the second division should be taken up, beginning with the most difficult, thus reversing the order observed in the first division.

Every school should open each day with singing, and, unless objection is made, the singing should be followed by the reading of a passage from the Scriptures, and by prayer. No teacher should permit a term of his school to be opened without these exercises. If he is himself unable to conduct them, some proper person in the district should be invited to be present at the opening of the school on the first day to invoke God's blessing upon the work about to be begun.

Teachers will find it convenient and useful to devote five minutes, immediately after the close of the opening exercises every morning, to a talk on the business of the day, and on matters in general, etc.

The classes in the alphabet should be first on the list for recitation. These may be followed by classes in spelling and reading, and these by classes in arithmetic, geography, history and the other sciences. Botany and geology should never be studied in the winter season in northern latitudes. No knowledge worth having can be imparted to children by teaching these sciences wholly within the barren limits of the school-room.

THE TIME-TABLE.

For the convenience of arranging a time-table and constructing a schedule, schools are classified as follows: Mixed schools, Graded schools, Academies and Colleges. Mixed schools are such as are kept in most of the rural districts, in which pupils of all grades study and recite in one room. Graded schools comprise all in which two or more teachers are employed, the pupils being classified according to the progress they have made. A time-table for a mixed school should fix a time for opening in the morning, times for recesses before noon, for a midday recess, for afternoon recesses and for closing. Thus the day will be divided into nearly equal parts. The teacher will then arrange his classes for recitations so as to occupy these periods of time to the best advantage; five minutes of time in each division should be reserved for miscellaneous duties.

The classes of small children should have short recitations after the opening of the school in the morning and immediately after each recess during the day. These pupils have not yet learned the art of preparing lessons; they require instruction. It is unwise to attempt to give them long lessons; short and frequent exercises will accomplish much more in the way of imparting knowledge, and at the same time will keep the little ones in better discipline.

Some of the more advanced pupils should recite before the first morning recess, and all of the more difficult recitations should be disposed of before twelve o'clock noon. Exercises in penmanship, composition, elocution, drawing and music should be reserved for the afternoon, but neither penmanship nor drawing lessons should be executed immediately after recess, as the nerves are then too unsteady for such work. The practice of devoting, at long intervals, half a day to exercises in composition and declamation rarely proves satisfactory. It will be found much more interesting to all, and much more profitable to the participants in these exercises, to divide the school into convenient classes, which can be made to rotate with each other, and with other exercises, as music lessons, drawing, etc., in such order as to consume a short interval near the close of each school-day.

After a table of exercises has been adopted it should be strictly adhered to in every particular, as the slightest variation therefrom destroys the confidence which its publication invokes, and thereby invites irregularity and confusion. If experience proves that changes in the schedule are necessary, their introduction should be duly announced, and the reasons for their adoption explained to the school. The introduction of recesses is intended to abolish the practice of passing in and out of the school-room by pupils during school-hours, as well as for purposes of recreation and exercise.

The ancient pail of water and tin-cup have long since been abolished from well-regulated schools, as nuisances. Every schoolhouse should be provided with water, so that at recess such pupils as desire may obtain it for drinking, but the pernicious practice of keeping water in the school-room, and of allowing the children during school-hours to leave their seats to obtain it, should not be permitted. Of course to this general rule with regard to leaving the room or partaking of water there will be occasionally exceptions, and of the propriety of these the teacher must be the judge, being careful always to err rather on the side of leniency.

CLASSIFICATION NECESSARY.

It is deemed unnecessary to present any arguments here in favor of classification. It is assumed that no teacher would be employed in any part of the United States, who does not recognize the necessity for a thorough classification of pupils in schools of every grade.

In the construction of classes it will always happen that dull and apt pupils are harnessed together. The effort to drag along a slow lad, and the attempt to goad him into the pace of his more apt companion, would be injurious; so likewise to retard the progress of the bright pupil, in order to keep him by the side of his dull classmate, would be equally improper. Other studies must, therefore, be provided for such as are able to do additional work. The apt pupils may be taken together to constitute a class in some additional branch of learning that can be introduced into the school; they will thus have less time to devote to each study, and yet all will be profitably employed.

FORMING CLASSES.

There is little danger of constructing classes too large in mixed schools. It rarely happens in the rural districts that any considerable number of pupils will be prepared to pursue the same studies at the same time. The general suggestion, therefore, that a teacher should arrange into the several classes, for which he has provided, all pupils who are able to pursue the branches of study laid down in the schedule, is deemed sufficient. This observation, however, applies only to the advanced pupils in our rural districts. The younger children must always be formed into small classes that will make short recitations in short lessons, whilst the advanced classes need recite but once a day in each study; in some of the less important branches, recitations may be given on alternate days by alternating classes with each other. Greater progress will be made, however, by daily recitations, though they be short, than by less frequent and longer recitations. It is advisable, therefore, to construct the order of exercises so as to provide as nearly as possible for daily recitations in every study.

ASSIGNING LESSONS.

In assigning lessons to each class, the average ability of the members must be taken as the measurement of the task to be imposed. The duller pupils must not be discouraged, and those who master their lessons must have enough to do. By patience and well-directed perseverance the teacher will soon be able to establish a general equality in the class, which will prove to be of great advantage throughout the term.

GRADED SCHOOLS.

The organization for graded schools is usually constructed by the local school-authorities, such as boards of control, school-directors and superintendents. Teachers are employed to take charge of special departments, and these departments have their classes and recitations, books and studies provided for in advance, independent of any action of the teachers. The proper organization of such schools, therefore, is treated of in another chapter.

CHAPTER V.

MANAGEMENT.

FOLLOWING the work of organizing is that of managing a school. The subject of School Government is not included in this division. The teacher is a legislator, an executive officer and an instructor. Before proceeding to the consideration of Methods of Instruction, it is proper to set forth a system for the management of the business of TEACHING.

THE FIRST LESSON.

After a school has been organized, the classes constructed, the times for recitation designated, as directed in the previous chapter, all things are in readiness for the pupils to enter upon the real work of the session. A lesson must now be assigned for each class. The teacher should be careful not to overtask his pupils in the beginning. Having first ascertained the average capacity of the members of the class and the average progress they have made, he should designate a place for beginning, and assign lessons entirely within the average comprehension and ability.

Incalculable advantage will accrue to both teacher and pupils, if the teacher will in advance of the time for meeting his class determine the place for beginning and the extent of the lesson to be given. He can then be prepared to give, in a conversation of five minutes' duration, a few practical hints to his class, suggesting a logical method of taking up the study, and briefly state what he will expect the class to accomplish in the recitation. This will establish pleasant relations between the teacher and his pupils, and will be an exhibition on his part of the possession of a thorough knowledge of the subject beyond what is found in the text-book. Recognizing this, the pupils will look to the teacher as a friend and helper in the labors that they are about to undertake.

It is essential to the existence of a proper relationship in the school-room, that the teacher shall not be regarded in any sense as a spy to detect the imperfections of the pupils, or a police officer to insist upon the performance of difficult tasks or to punish delinquencies. By beginning work as has been indicated the teacher assumes the position of an instructor, he establishes himself in the confidence of his pupils by giving evidence that he is able to teach. All this is essential to the success of the school.

These general directions, though they are emphasized in their importance in the case of classes coming for the first time before a teacher may with advantage and profit be adopted for the introduction of every new subject that is encountered in the progress of study. To illustrate: suppose a class in arithmetic is about to enter upon the study of *proportion.* The time for the first recitation should be wholly consumed by the teacher in explanation of the subject. The members of a proportion should be written on the blackboard, and their relation to each other fully explained, in a method suited to the comprehension of every pupil. This done, the teacher may write upon the board a simple example, as, "If twelve hats cost twenty-four dollars, what will seven hats cost?" The laws of proportion having been explained to the class, the teacher proceeds to construct from this problem a proportion in accordance with the principles he has already laid down. There are three members of the proportion given, and a fourth is required. Now, this required term will be the answer to the question—namely, the price of seven hats—and will be expressed in dollars. It is evident, therefore, that the fourth term of the proportion will be dollars, and as the third term must be of the same denomination as the fourth, it also must be dollars; therefore, write twenty-four dollars on the blackboard as the third term of the proportion. The third term is the price of twelve hats; the fourth term when found will be the price of seven hats; consequently, the fourth term will be smaller than the third. According to the principles of proportion already explained, if the fourth term is smaller than the third, the second term must be smaller than the first. Hence, write seven hats for the second term and twelve hats for the first term. It is not necessary here to explain the methods of solving proportions.

If the teacher has been clear in his demonstration, his class will be able, from the illustration given, to construct a proportion for every example found in any ordinary arithmetic under this rule, and having thus acquired by the process of deduction the rule for the solution of problems involving these principles, this rule will be part of the pupils' positive knowledge, not to be forgotten, as mere memorized matter very often is.

Suppose it is the geography class, and that it is about to enter upon the study of one of the grand divisions—as, for example, Europe. The teacher should now have before him a map of the world. Using the knowledge the class has already acquired in the study of other grand divisions, the teacher should state briefly the historical relations between what has been studied and what is about to be studied. If the class has passed over that portion of the book which treats of the western continent, as is usual in geographies published in the United States, it will be profitable to call attention to the manner in which America was discovered, and how it was settled by people from Europe; how Europe, prior to that time, had been settled by people from Asia, thus showing the class that it is entering upon the study of the geography of an older settled country than that of which it had previously studied. The general characteristics of the government, the people, the political subdivisions and the characters of the nations and of the people inhabiting these subdivisions should be outlined, contrasting what is to be with what has been studied, in such manner as will tend to arouse the curiosity and fix the attention of the pupils upon the subject before them. The general geographical relation of the new with the old should be noted, together with such matters of general interest as tend to show the connection between them, as may occur to the mind of the teacher.

Suppose, again, that the subject to be taken

up by the class is botany; the teacher should be prepared in advance with specimens of plants, seeds and flowers gathered from the neighboring fields or woods. He should explain the nature and scope of the science of botany, note the pleasures that will arise during, and the benefits that may result from, its study. Exhibiting to the class the specimens before him, he will be able to show, that on some plants the leaves grow on the stem opposite each other, that on others they come out on opposite sides alternately, and that in others they grow in circles or whorls; that plants differ in the form of their roots, some having straight, slender, branching roots, and others having bulbs, and that they differ in the form and structure of their fruit. The general peculiarities of the flower should also attract attention. In some there is but one petal, in others, two, three, four and five, or a great many. The class may be told that plants are arranged in great families, and that these are subdivided into classes, genera, species and varieties, indicated by their several similarities and differences.

These illustrations are sufficient to explain the general method. It may be readily applied in every branch of study introduced into the public schools, and the time allotted for the first recitation of each class in any subject cannot be more profitably consumed. The lesson previously determined upon by the teacher may then be assigned, and in the preparation of that lesson for recitation, each pupil will be pleased to find, that he is entering upon the work of discovering the facts, that have been indicated and clothed with new interest by the preliminary remarks of the teacher.

It will readily be imagined how much more eagerly pupils will enter upon the study of a subject that has been so pleasantly unfolded to them, than would be the case if the same had been harshly thrust at them with an implied indifference, as if to say, "There! take that and make the most of it."

By some educators the idea is entertained that the acquisition of knowledge must not be made easy and agreeable. Upon all such, of course, these suggestions are lost, but to that large class of intelligent, educated and conscientious men and women, engaged in the management of schools throughout the country, and who are putting forth earnest efforts to elevate and methodize the business of school-teaching, this practice is commended with the full confidence, that wherever it is intelligently applied it will give satisfaction to both teacher and pupil. When the study of a subject shall have been concluded, the teacher may, by a succinct and well-digested review of the matter gone over, greatly assist the members of the class in fixing upon the mind, in logical order, the leading facts in such manner as will enable them to grasp the whole subject in a single effort.

NUMBER OF STUDIES.

The number of branches that should be studied, at the same time, will to some extent depend upon the capacity of the pupil. The universal experience in the best schools, both in this country and in Europe, has settled upon the assigning of three studies as the course which may be pursued with the most profit to the student. Reading, writing, declamation, composition, music, drawing, and the like, are not included in the catalogue of full studies. These are taken up in convenient order in addition to the three studies that require more time and closer application. Occasionally pupils will be found so slow of comprehension as to be unable to keep up their work in three classes. These may be allowed to take but two regular studies, and to consume their time in the somewhat physical exercises as above indicated. Others will possess an aptness to acquire knowledge that will enable them to take up four, or even five, of the regular studies, in addition to the ordinary complement of those branches requiring little or no preparation.

The tendency in most public schools is to load down the pupils with too much work. There are few graded schools in the villages and cities throughout the United States, in which pupils are not required to recite in from ten to fifteen, or even a greater number, of branches of study every week. This, in every sense, is a pernicious practice tending to confusion of thought, and is prejudicial to sound mental discipline. It is far better to take up three studies, and to prosecute them with reasonable rapidity, and when the limits of a public-school course shall be reached to take up three others, and thus, in the same time, fully as many branches can be studied, without the confusing of facts and philosophy, but in a manner that will enable the pupil to obtain a distinct knowledge of each science, and to use the facts of each in the elucidation of the principles of others.

THREE STUDIES ENOUGH.

If it is true, as experience teaches, that three studies, at the utmost, afford sufficient work for young men in the colleges and universities, it is much more true of the pupils of tender ages in the mixed schools of the rural districts, and of the graded schools of villages and cities. No man who has enjoyed the advantages of a college education, and who has attained that culture which creates within him an active sympathy for the injured of every class, can look with complacency upon the troops of girls and boys passing to and from school, loaded down with satchels and packages of books, that a young man at college could, by no act of persuasion, be forced to totter under. On the college *campus* an armful of books is indicative of feeble-mindedness. It would be uncharitable to judge the girls and boys of the public schools by this rule, but it is true, that the system of education which induces this book-lugging practice is the chief source of that feeble-mindedness, which shows itself in the general obtuseness of intellect with which every effort at essential progress is so obstinately confronted. Whilst, therefore, the claim of scientific study is urged upon the attention of the public-school authorities, the necessity for such an arrangement of classes as will provide for the studying of all branches in groups of three is insisted upon.

THOROUGHNESS NECESSARY.

Thoroughness in the work of every day is the key which unlocks that mystery of success, whereby well-qualified teachers lead their classes in regular succession, through numerous branches of learning by prosecuting but a small number at the same time. Thus, instead of giving one term to "mental arithmetic," another term to "written arithmetic," and a third to "higher arithmetic," let the subject be taken up and disposed of in one or two sessions. Let grammar and geography be treated in the same manner; then, with this put behind him, the pupil will advance to other branches of study, in which the principles and formulas previously learned are applied, extended and utilized. A teacher, who understands the subject of arithmetic and the art of teaching it, will be able to so instruct his class, by going over the subject once, that it will not be necessary to drag the dull length of that subject through the numerous terms of the whole period of school-life. Algebra, geometry, trigonometry, natural philosophy, chemistry, geography, geology, botany and most other branches of study, that can be pursued in the public schools, or in higher institutions, employ the principles and apply the processes of arithmetic, and they furnish sufficient opportunity for review. The study of abstract principles is a means of disciplining the mind, but the use of those principles, in the search for knowledge in other paths, establishes them as part of the working power of the mind. The study of history affords the best reviewing grounds wherein to display the facts of geography. Botany and geology review both history and geography.

HIGHEST RESULTS REQUIRED.

A teacher who was devoted to the study of arithmetic, chiefly because he understood nothing else, with countenance glowing with imagined victory, exclaimed, "Do you pretend to say that a class of boys and girls derives no benefit from the exercises found in our higher arithmetics?" To this the very pertinent answer was given: "It is not enough that pupils shall merely derive benefit from any exercise; there is a greater question to be settled, namely: Is the time of the pupil so occupied as to secure to himself the greatest possible advantage?" That teacher who is content simply because he is doing good, certainly falls very far short of the discharge of his duty to the public, more especially so if, by the employment of different methods, much more could be accomplished in the same time. A farmer may purchase a fertilizer at a distance of five miles from his home at a cost of fifty dollars per ton; he may consume time in laying it upon his fields, spreading it upon the surface and working it into the soil, and will be profited thereby. By going the same distance in an opposite direction, he could have purchased an article vastly superior to that which he is content to use; by the employment of the same time and labor, therefore, he might have added a much higher degree of productiveness to the soil, and might have reaped threefold the benefits that were realized from the use of the inferior fertilizer. Is he a judicious farmer, who is content to use a compound, simply because it increases the fertility of his soil, though at the same cost he might obtain far greater results by the use of another? School authorities and teachers, employed in cultivating the public mind, have a duty to perform infinitely more delicate in its nature and far-reaching in its results, than has he who expends his efforts on the rude elements of the earth. It requires research and deliberation to discover and select, and it requires courage to apply that which is best. But until they are reasonably assured that the results of each school-term are the highest attainable, by the means at their command, neither the board of education, the teacher, the pupils nor the great public interested in the success of the people's school should cease from efforts to lift up, expand and perfect the system.

STUDY.

To study the lesson is the next business in order. In this the teacher has a twofold duty to perform: First, to prepare himself for the recitation; secondly, to so direct the efforts of his pupils in their studies, as will enable them to accomplish the greatest amount of work in the shortest space of time. It will be of great advantage to the school if, at the beginning of the term, the teacher will explain, in a general way, the nature and object of study. Upon the organization of each class more specific directions should be given, having special reference to the branch of learning about to be taken up by the class. In the five minutes after the opening of school each day, set apart for miscellaneous matters, the teacher may frequently remind the whole school of his instructions on this subject.

THE OBJECT OF STUDY.

Study has for its immediate object the acquisition of knowledge. The act of accumulating facts previously unknown is of itself a pure source of pleasure, and the consciousness of the possession of knowledge gives birth to soul-inspiring reflections, among the most delightful experienced by mankind. In all of its departments Nature has laid up great stores of original and independent truths. These are discovered and brought forth by human efforts, and by human efforts they are arranged in natural order and combined under natural laws, in such manner as to constitute science. The pleasure arising from the discovery and combination of these truths in nature, amply repays the labor and efforts put forth by the student.

UTILITY OF KNOWLEDGE.

Apart from the pure gratification that arises from the act of accumulating knowledge, there is the idea of usefulness attached to every fact that is acquired. A knowledge of the simple processes of arithmetic is useful in the ordinary business transactions of society. Knowledge of the facts of history and of geography enables one to read intelligently the news of the day, and to discourse upon it understandingly. A knowledge of the elementary principles of chemistry, natural philosophy, physical geography, botany, mineralogy, and the like, is of practical use to the farmer, the doctor of medicine, the traveler, the navigator—in short, to a man in almost any of the pursuits, whether commercial, manufacturing, agricultural or professional—and this relation of school-day study to the business of after-life should in no sense be ignored or under-estimated. It will stand as an incentive to study with many, on whom the idea of pleasure and discipline would have no effect or weight. What to one is a sordid and unworthy motive, to another may stand as the end and aim of his loftiest ambition. The utility of knowledge should, therefore, be duly set forth for the edification of such as are weak.

STUDY USEFUL FOR DISCIPLINE.

Study is useful to discipline the powers of the mind. The musician, whose fingers touch with rapidity and marvelous accuracy and delicacy the keys of the instrument, was once but a clumsy beginner. By continued systematic practice he has attained a perfection, which commands the admiration of all lovers of this art. The powers of the mind are in reference to their developments not unlike the powers of the body. They are perfected by discipline, and this discipline is attained through systematic and logical mental effort. Pupils must not, therefore, be allowed to blunder along as best they may in the preparation of their lessons. Feebleness of mind is inseparably connected with obtuseness of sense. Whatever method of training, therefore, sharpens the senses, must inevitably strengthen the mind. One of the first efforts, therefore, in the school-room should be so directed as to accustom the children to the proper exercise of the senses. This under all circumstances will prove to be the most effectual means of developing the mental powers. From early infancy a child acquires knowledge by observation. At first this observation proceeds in an undirected, hap-hazard sort of way, without system or purpose. It is the duty of the teacher to systematize and regulate these exercises of the senses. If bungling methods are employed, or the pupil is allowed to proceed without method, the exercise of his senses will soon be embarrassed, limited and altogether arrested; a dull, feeble-minded man or woman will be the result. But if, on the other hand, this natural propensity to acquire knowledge by observation is, by easy process, brought under proper discipline, the first great duty of the teacher is discharged.

Precisely here is the occasion and the reason for introducing the study of the material sciences into the public schools. The elementary facts of the sciences are acquired through the senses, and should therefore be presented to the pupil at the time these faculties are most active. At a later period, when Judgment, which arranges, and Reason, which combines, have been developed, these facts of science will be arranged and combined, and thus philosophy, the soul of science, will be evolved. These facts, gathered in early years through the operation of the senses, and this philosophy, evolved by Reason, whereby facts are brought together in natural order, constitute science. The work of observing and combining is study; if this is logically carried forward, the highest discipline of all the faculties of the mind will be attained. As by discipline the musician is enabled to use his physical powers to produce the highest effects in art, as the smith, by discipline, is enabled to direct with precision the stroke of his hammer, and as the sportsman, by discipline, acquires the ability to balance with absolute accuracy his rifle, so the student, by discipline, is enabled to bring under perfect control all the powers of his mind, to be used promptly, accurately and efficiently at any instant, and for a definite purpose. As playing ball, swinging on ropes and vaulting on bars give muscular power, but no efficiency, to the musician, the mechanic or the artisan, so unguided or misdirected efforts of the intellectual faculties may result in the accumulation of facts, may store the mind with knowledge without disciplining the faculties in such manner as to give efficiency to mental action, or ability to logically pursue principles to practical results. It is, therefore, of importance that the habits and methods of study in the public schools shall be so formed as not only to store the mind of the pupil with facts, but rather to accustom the mind to work systematically with a purpose which from the beginning seeks an end. By these means, and not otherwise, study will serve the purposes of discipline.

STUDYING A LESSON.

The subject of study having been determined upon, its nature and scope explained to the class and the lesson assigned, the immediate work in hand for the class, is the preparation of the lesson for recitation. The act of studying, combined with that of reciting, should result in making the facts and the principles which connect them, as set forth in the lesson, the property of the pupil. Studying the lesson is first in order. It is assumed that a text-book, with all the subjects arranged in logical order and expressed in concise and plain language, is in the possession of each pupil, and that a portion of the text has been assigned for study. The pupil should read over carefully the whole lesson, so as to obtain a general idea of its scope. Each point should then be taken up and attentively considered. The mind of the student should be undividedly fixed upon each fact and circumstance in the lesson, and these should be, one after the other, thoroughly mastered, and, finally, all should be connected in the mind in their natural order. Thus will be generated the power to express, in the pupil's own language, the gist of the subject under consideration. If the attempt be made to extract the meaning of the lesson by simply reading over and re-reading, and endeavoring to contemplate the whole by a single effort, the result will be failure.

Occasionally pupils are possessed of such aptness of comprehension that they acquire knowledge with little effort, but the great majority must labor systematically and patiently, in order thoroughly to comprehend the truths set forth in the text. The method, therefore, here recommended, is—

1st. View the whole subject.

2d. Take up item by item and master each distinct and separate fact.

3d. Grasp the connecting principles, which combine these facts, by contemplating them in the order in which they are set down in the text-book.

4th. Give expression to what has been learned.

This done, the pupil is prepared for the recitation. The subject may then be laid aside, and another lesson in another branch of learning may be taken up and treated in a similar manner.

In no case should a pupil sit down to the study of several lessons without having first definitely arranged, in what order they shall be taken up, and what time shall be devoted to the study of each. The same order should be observed daily, without variance from a written time-table previously prepared and kept convenient for reference.

The student who studies a lesson only enough to obtain a general and superficial idea of its principles, and then takes up a second and a third and treats them in the same way, will never acquire definite knowledge on any subject, and will grow up into habits of hesitation in speech, uncertainty in thought and inefficiency in action. Thorough comprehension gives directness and clearness of expression. Uncertainty of knowledge gives hesitation and confusion of expression. A teacher observant of this principle will detect, in the utterances of the pupils at recitation, whether the subject of the lesson is comprehended.

USES OF RECITATION.

The recitation exercise serves two purposes:

1st. It discovers to the teacher whether the subject under consideration is comprehended by the members of the class.

2d. It fixes in the mind of the pupil more permanently all the knowledge evolved in the study of the text.

ON CONDUCTING RECITATIONS.

A teacher, who is competent for the post he occupies, will not permit the recitation exercise to be one in which the pupils simply recite what they have learned, but he will enlarge on the subject by noting collateral facts, and by citing applications and uses of the knowledge acquired by the class. Let it be ever kept in view, that the class-book is but a *text*-book; the text should be suggestive to both teacher and pupil. By the use of books of reference and comprehensive treatises on the subject of the text-book, a teacher will be enabled to obtain much interesting matter relating to the subject of each lesson, not found in the concise treatises in the hands of the pupils; from this full store he can draw, daily, with eminent advantage to himself and to the pupils under his charge.

What has elsewhere been said may be repeated with emphasis here, that no effort of the teacher will conduce so much to good government, to establish confidence and to winning the respect of the school and of the whole neighborhood, as this ability to enlarge upon every theme called up in recitation. A teacher, content to sit in his chair and hear the recitation of the class, without making such intelligent comment as will enlarge the store of knowledge and fix it more durably in the minds of the pupils, is utterly unfit for his position. This is true of teachers in mixed schools, in graded schools, in high schools, and in academies, colleges and universities. For, whether the recitation be in the history of the United States in a country school, or whether it be in chemistry at the academy, or in Greek verse at the college, a teacher, who mechanically and passively listens to what pupils have to say, simply correcting dates in history and facts in chemistry, or construction in Greek, is making the very worst use of the pupil's time. If he has no collateral, corroborative or strengthening matter to present, he lacks the requisite ability to fill the position he is occupying. If, on the other hand, he is possessed of such matter and fails to bring it forward, he is guilty of criminal neglect, and should be summarily dismissed from the place he so badly fills.

In the study of the lesson, the chief effort rests with the student, but in the recitation the onus is upon the teacher. As soon as a pupil shall have gone far enough in the recitation to satisfy the teacher, that the subject has been carefully studied and the matter set forth in the text fully mastered, it becomes his duty to enlarge upon the text. Thus the recitation will always be looked forward to by the pupil as an agreeable and profitable exercise. Too often now, owing to the prevalence of illy-conceived methods, a pupil approaches a recitation with hesitation and fear. He receives no benefit; no new facts are brought out, and his knowledge is not enlarged; he is simply puzzled, annoyed and vexed by hard questions, invented by stupid authors and asked by incompetent teachers.

The school authorities and the Normal School faculties should see that this method is abolished and the more reasonable one, as explained above, substituted.

FORCIBLE ILLUSTRATIONS.

In every school many forcible illustrations may be improvised by the teacher. In the study of botany, plants and vegetables are at hand, and may be exhibited to the class for demonstration of facts. In the study of anatomy and physiology, bones, muscles, joints and other parts of animals slaughtered in the neighborhood may be exhibited. For the class in geology, rocks from different formations may be found convenient to almost every schoolhouse. In natural philosophy, many simple contrivances with ball, string, levers, springs and the like may be constructed by the ingenious teacher. In history, many incidents and interesting stories, suggested by the text, may be related for the instruction of the class. Thus, by devices innumerable, an active, intelligent teacher will, day after day, enlarge upon the text, bringing stores of knowledge to his class, for which he will be repaid an hundredfold in the affections of his pupils and in the enlarged respect and good-will of the patrons of his school.

CHAPTER VI.

METHODS OF INSTRUCTION.

NATIONAL PECULIARITIES.

THE population of the United States comprises English, German, French, Italian, Spanish, Swedish, Norwegians, Dutch, Irish, Scotch and Welsh people. From the period of the early settlements in America to the present, emigrants have been received from all of the different nations of the world. The nations of Europe have furnished very considerable contributions to the populations of most of the States. These have brought with them their peculiarities of life and language, and these peculiarities have impressed themselves upon the institutions of the United States. Frequently public-school authorities provide for teaching school in foreign languages. In some places, in addition to the English schools, there are also established German schools, French schools, Swede schools, Dutch schools or Welsh schools. In those places where the people of any nation or country have settled in close communities, schools in their own lan guages are necessary, but in a country where all business, public and private, is transacted in the English language, the teaching in the public schools should be in that language.

Families coming from Germany or from France, Holland, Sweden or Norway, experience great inconvenience in the transaction of business in America, and it would seem to be exceedingly short-sighted to establish schools so as to perpetuate that inconvenience, by transmitting it to the children, growing up in an English-speaking country. A much wiser course would be to require the children to attend the English schools, and to there learn the use of the language that is prevalent in the land of their adoption.

When the children of foreign parentage are found in the public schools, the teacher has imposed upon him a peculiar task. He must correct the faulty articulation of those who have been in the habit of speaking a foreign language, and bring such pupils to accustom their organs of speech to the enunciation of the elementary sounds of the English language. This will be accomplished by systematic and often-repeated exercises.

FOREIGNERS AND ENGLISH ARTICULATION.

The most successful method known to practical teachers, by which to overcome the peculiarities of children accustomed to speak foreign languages, is to drill thoroughly in the elementary sounds. In order to apply this method effectually, it will be necessary to study the correct use of the organs of speech, and classify the elementary sounds with reference to the organs employed in giving them utterance. Thus, a teacher will be able to show clearly the difference between the manner of using these organs in a faulty and in a correct enunciation. For example, a German boy, in all probability, will pronounce the word *thing*, *sing*. The difference is in the articulation of the first elementary sound in the word. It is the difference between the sound of *th* and *s*. The pupil must be taught to understand that, in producing the sound of *s*, he places the tip of his tongue against the roof of his mouth, that in uttering the sound of *th*, he places his tongue between his teeth. If, therefore, when he attempts to pronounce the word *thing*, he begins by placing the tip of his tongue between his teeth, it will be impossible for him to utter it in the *s* sound, as *sing*.

It is also very common for children born of foreign parents to confound the sounds represented by *w* and *v*. If the pupil distinguishes how differently the organs of speech are used in the utterance of these sounds, he will have no difficulty in giving them correct utterance. Thus, in producing the sound of *w*, the lips project as they do in uttering the sound of *oo;* whereas, in giving utterance to the sound represented by *v*, the upper teeth are brought in a gentle pressure upon the lower lip; with the lip and teeth thus brought together it is impossible to produce the sound represented by *w*.

This subject will be treated of more at length in connection with the instructions in the elementary sounds. The object of introducing so much of it here is to enforce the statement that, by teaching the proper use of the organs of speech in the enunciation of sounds used in the English language, the child embarrassed by faulty pronunciation will be enabled most speedily to overcome the force of habit. This will require perseverance on the part of both teacher and pupil, but the effect will soon be observed, and the final result will be, that those children who, because of the habits of childhood, were compelled to make special efforts to drill in the elementary sounds, will grow up to be more perfect in their articulation and pronunciation of the language, than those who were, at the beginning, esteemed their more fortunate associates.

ELOCUTION.

Elocution, as here applied, includes the learning of the Alphabet, Spelling, Reading and Declamation. It is considered as first among the branches of learning to be taught in the public schools, chiefly for the reason, that it is always first in order, and will doubtless remain so, among those studies that are taught from books. The subdivisions will be taken up in the order named.

METHODS OF TEACHING THE ALPHABET.

Two methods for teaching the alphabet are in general use. One is called the Letter Method and the other the Word Method.

The Letter Method is that in which the twenty-six letters of the alphabet are taught separately, one after the other.

The Word Method is that in which pupils are first taught to recognize and pronounce words; these, by analysis, are separated into their elements, and these elements being letters, a child is taught to distinguish them from each other, and to name them.

In the Letter Method, the alphabet may be taught by means of a number of devices.

1st. *Teaching the Alphabet from a Book.*—In

times past it was almost a universal practice to teach the Alphabet to children singly. A child was called up with a primer or A-B-C book in hand, and the teacher, pointing to the letters beginning at *a* and ending with *z*, would name the letter and require the child to repeat it after him; or, beginning at the letter *z*, the Alphabet was "said backward" to *a*. As the child progressed in these exercises, the teacher would point to some one letter in the Alphabet and require the child to name it; or, varying the exercises, a child would be required to point to some letter which the teacher named, as *o*, *x*, *g*, *w*. In some schools this practice still obtains. It is unquestionably the most severe and uninteresting to the child of all the methods yet devised. It requires the teacher to give his whole attention to each child separately. There can be no classification, and, consequently, no rivalry, because there is no class. All the advantages of classification are lost. There can be no interest excited in the minds of the pupils. The exercise is arbitrary, and even after the child shall have learned to name the twenty-six letters of the English alphabet, it will generally be so utterly ignorant of the use of this learning that it is very likely to question "whether it is worth while to endure so much in order to learn so little."

It is possible to so vary the exercises as to greatly improve on the system of saying the A B C forward and backward, as was formerly the general practice. The successful teacher will, by questions and little combinations, greatly facilitate the labors of the child in its efforts to memorize these twenty-six arbitrary characters. It will be wiser, however, to abandon this method altogether, and to adopt one that is more practical in its application and fruitful in its results.

2d. *Teaching the Alphabet from Charts.*—A series of Charts, varying in the size of the letters printed on them and in the simplicity of combinations, may be used with great advantage in teaching the Alphabet. Chart No. 1 should contain the twenty-six letters of the Alphabet printed in large plain type. The margins of this Chart should be occupied by smaller letters, promiscuously arranged, so that several impressions of each letter might be found on the Chart. The teacher may now be supposed to have his A-B-C class before him for recitation. The Chart is so suspended as to be easily seen by each member of the class. He points to some one of the large letters and pronounces its name. At first, one of the plain, distinct letters, as O, A or I, should be selected. "This is A;" let the class repeat the name of the letter after the teacher. If the teacher will draw in chalk on the blackboard the letter A, and describe its parts so as to attract the attention of the pupils to its construction, both the form and the name of the letter will be more rapidly and durably impressed upon the mind. After this form has been made familiar, the teacher should ask of the class, "Can you find another A on the Chart?" Some of the pupils will find one, some two and others three or four, and thus rivalry is at once excited, and the attention of the whole class directed to the Chart.

The use of the blackboard in connection with the Chart will increase the interest in and the force of the instruction given. As the class progresses the teacher may leave the letter drawn on the blackboard half finished and require the pupils to complete it, or he may draw a faulty letter and require the pupils to state the difference between it and the correct form on the Chart.

Chart No. 2 should contain simple combinations of the letters of the Alphabet, in such manner as to spell the names of familiar objects, as AX, OX, CAT, RAT, DOG, COW, FORK, HORSE. The number of these may be increased by the use of the blackboard. The class can be exercised in naming the letters found in these combinations, and in pronouncing the words thus formed. A familiar talk respecting the objects represented by these words will interest the pupils in the spelling of their names. On this Chart there must also be such combinations as will aid the pupil in learning readily, that different sounds are represented by the same letter. Thus, *a* in the word *cat* has one sound, and in the word *bale* it has another sound; *o* in the word *ox* has one sound, and in the word *old* it has another sound; that *i* has one sound in *bite*, and another in *lip*. These, it is true, are, to the child, arbitrary distinctions, but they will soon be learned by force of habit and retained upon the very impressible memory of childhood.

Chart No. 3 can be printed in smaller type, and may contain longer words. These should be arranged with reference to the sound of the vowels used.

Chart No. 4 should be arranged for drill on the elementary sounds of both vowels and consonants. This chart may be used with profit throughout the whole course of elocutionary training in the school, from the A-B-C class to the classes in declamation and composition. Teachers possessing different degrees of skill and genius for teaching, will vary the exercises on these Charts in almost innumerable ways, with profit to their classes. The direction here is simply, that no teacher should be content to hear the same lessons repeatedly, without variation; he should exercise his ingenuity to vary the instruction so as to give new interest and to create expectation for every recitation.

TEACHING THE ALPHABET WITH LETTER BLOCKS.

The apparatus for teaching the Alphabet from blocks consists of twenty-six, or more blocks containing letters painted or pasted on them of such size as to be easily distinguished. Each pupil should possess a set of these blocks, and each set of blocks should contain the complete Alphabet, with duplicates of the vowels. In order to conduct a recitation with blocks, the class should be arranged around a table of convenient height for the children when standing. The pupils should place their blocks before them on the table, and the teacher, having a set for his own use, may take a block in his hand and hold it in a position that all the class can see it; he will give the name of the letter on it, and then require the pupils to find the same letter in their respective sets. Thus several of the leading letters will be made familiar in form and name. The teacher may ask a pupil to find one of these letters, as O; another may find A; another X; another T; and so on. As a little more progress is made by repeating these exercises, which should be duly varied every day, these letters can be combined in words containing two or three letters each. Thus the teacher may take in his hand the three letters, B, O, Y, or he may draw these three letters on the blackboard and then require each member of the class to select them from the blocks. That these three letters combined spell the word *boy* should be fully explained, and so enforced that the children will understand it. Other similar combinations may be formed, and thus the children, as it were in a game of play, will, with eagerness and delight, shuffle their blocks into words that will become familiar.

If the teacher will write on the blackboard the names of animals or other familiar objects, the pupils will rapidly select from their blocks letters corresponding to those on the blackboard, and will thus construct words. In like manner, by the use of blocks, children may be taught to count and to distinguish the forms of numerals.

TEACHING THE ALPHABET ON SLATE AND BLACKBOARD.

Another, and in some respects the most successful, method of teaching the Alphabet, is to require every child to have a small slate and pencil. Pupils will, in an incredibly short time, acquire the ability to draw the letters of the Alphabet, and to print words. No other exercise will so distinctly and durably fix in the mind the form of the letters as that of drawing them. The letter to be drawn by the children, in their seats, should be printed upon the blackboard by the teacher, or, what is better, the teacher should have a set of cards, each having on it a large letter; one of these can be so placed that all the children engaged in the exercise can distinctly see it. The letters most simple in form, as I, H, A, X, O, should be taken up first. Combinations of the simple letters can be made, and words spelled on the slates by the children, before the formation of letters more complicated in form is undertaken. The slate and pencil may be used, not only to teach the Alphabet, but also to teach drawing, and to relieve in a pleasant manner the somewhat irksome duties of a child in school, who, too often, is required to sit in quiet idleness for an hour or more, without rest or change, and is then called up for a five minutes' recitation to say the A B C.

The time was when children, who sketched horses, articles of school-furniture, doll-babies, chairs and animals on their slates, were punished for misconduct. Such barbarism has been banished from all properly-conducted schools, and the propensities of childhood are taken advantage of, both for matters of discipline in reference to order and in teaching the primary lessons in school. This is a much more reasonable course, and should be everywhere adopted. Children with slates and pencils in their possession are rarely idle or mischievous if the teacher, by sketches on the blackboard, or by charts containing the letters of the alphabet and simple lessons in drawing, will furnish exercise for the ingenuity, and opportunity for the amusement of the little ones, who may thus be educated without violence.

Vastly better than a rigid adherence to any one of these methods is such a combination of all of them as will give variety and interest even to the A-B-C class. Books, charts, blocks, slates and the blackboard should all be used to amuse and interest the children, for that learning, the acquisition of which is made attractive by numerous pleasant devices, is always most profitable to the young.

THE WORD METHOD.

By observation children become familiar with numerous objects, and by imitation they acquire a knowledge of the names of these objects. To a very considerable extent children acquire the use of language by imitation. The word method of teaching the alphabet is based upon this circumstance. Familiar objects, or pictures of such objects, are placed before the child, and the name drawn upon the blackboard, or printed on a chart or in a book, is pointed out. Thus the word method may be taught by the use of the blackboard, from charts or from books.

TEACHING THE ALPHABET FROM THE BLACKBOARD.

In using the blackboard for giving instruction to a class in the Alphabet by the Word Method, the teacher takes in his hand a familiar object, as a HAT. He prints in plain letters the name of the object on the blackboard, and the children are taught to associate that word with the object. The word is composed of three parts; these parts the teacher may write separately upon the board. The first of these elements the teacher tells the class is named H, the second is named A, and the third is named T—that is, one H, one A and one T, placed in the order in which they are written on the board, make the word which is pronounced HAT. This fact, by the aid of numerous illustrations, must be made clear to the class.

The teacher may take a small boy from the class and place him on the platform by the blackboard, and write on the board, BOY. He says to the class, "This word on the blackboard is BOY." The class is made to associate the word and the object with each other. The word is then decomposed into its letters, and the names of the letters are given and repeated until they will readily be remembered by the class. In like manner a TOP, a BALL, a KITE, a BOOK and other objects may be associated with the words that stand for them, and the several words may be separated into their elements, and the names of the letters may be learned by the class. The object may be removed and the words remain on the board. The class should then be required to pronounce the words, and also to name the letters that compose them. These exercises may be extended and varied at the will of the teacher as necessity may require.

TEACHING THE ALPHABET BY THE USE OF CHARTS.

The teacher is supposed to be provided with several Charts.

Chart No. 1 should contain pictures of the most familiar animals, and other objects with short names, such as Cat, Dog, Hen, Robin, Horse, Pig, Cow, Hat, Chain, Top, Kite, and such other illustrations as the size of the Chart will admit of. The pictures should be sufficiently large and distinct to be readily distinguished, and the name of each should be printed beneath it in large plain letters. The children in the A-B-C class must now be instructed to associate these pictures and these names with the animals, or objects they represent. They must be taught that both picture and word represent the same thing. The words may then be separated and each letter considered by itself, and the name of each committed to memory. The children will soon learn that the word and the picture, CAT, represent a familiar animal, and that the word is composed of C, A, T. On the margin of this card the words should be printed in columns, apart from the pictures, and the children should be required to select the word belonging to each picture, to pronounce it and to name the letters that compose it.

Chart No. 2 should be an advance on No. 1—that is, animals and objects having longer names may be placed on it. In all other respects it is the same as No. 1, and the manner of using it is also the same.

Chart No. 3 may introduce words not representing animals, as verbs, adjectives, prepositions and words that may be used in constructing short sentences. Pictures may be drawn to represent the idea set forth in the sentence, as, The boy has a kite. Boys play ball. Girls jump the rope. Cows eat grass. This idea may be enlarged upon by the use of the blackboard.

Chart No. 4 should introduce the distinction in the elementary sounds represented by the letters, and should be so constructed as to be convenient for drilling the class in the elements in a manner similar to that described under the Letter Method of teaching the Alphabet from charts.

TEACHING THE ALPHABET FROM BOOKS.

To teach the Alphabet in the Word Method from books, each member of the class should possess an illustrated primer, in which there are numerous pictures of animals and familiar objects, similar to those described on Charts Nos. 1 and 2. All who are beginning to learn the Alphabet should be arranged in a class and brought before the teacher at the same time. Some picture should be selected for the lesson, and the word and the picture should be associated, so that the children will understand that both represent the same thing, and that in naming the picture they are pronouncing the word. If the picture is that of an OX, let the idea be enforced that the picture and the little word of two letters represent the animal. The word may be drawn on the blackboard, and the children will recognize it there, as the same as that found in the book. So with the names of other objects pictured in the primer; they should be transferred to the blackboard by the teacher, so that the children may become accustomed to recognize the name apart from the picture.

The teacher may assign one or more of the pictures in the book for a lesson, and instruct the children to print the name on the slate, and if they will also draw the picture of the object, or animal, on the slate, it is still better. Indeed, no more agreeable or profitable exercise could be devised for the period of Alphabet studying, than that of transferring to the slate the pictures that are found in the child's primer.

SLATES FOR CHILDREN.

Whatever method may be adopted, and whatever the mode of procedure under the method, the use of the slate, by the children studying the Alphabet, is insisted upon as indispensable to good order in school and rapid progress in acquiring a knowledge of the forms, names, sounds and uses of the letters of the Alphabet. By numerous simple lessons from the blackboard, from charts or from books, the teacher may find business for the little fingers, amusement for the little brains and pleasure for the little hearts, that would otherwise be in mischief, idleness or pain. Let it, therefore, be set down as one of the indispensable requisites in an infant class, that every member shall possess a slate and pencil, and in the use of these give the largest liberty. That teacher, who so combines parts of all these methods and devices, and adapts them to the necessities of the cases before him, will be most successful.

ORTHOGRAPHY.

There are two general methods of teaching spelling. These arise from the nature of the circumstances presented, and the object to be attained. First, there is given the *form* of words, and from these the pupil is required to obtain the pronunciation, or, secondly, the *pronunciation* may be given and the pupil required to produce the form.

SPELLING FROM SIGHT.

The first method here considered is that in which the pupil analyses the word into its elementary sounds for purposes of pronunciation. This is the usual method pursued in the schools. The primer, the spelling-book, the reader and charts supply lists of words. The pronunciation of these is to be learned by naming the letters composing each syllable, pronouncing the syllable, and then uniting the sounds of the syllables into the whole word. Where this method is pursued, pupils should be required to spell the words by first naming the letters, and after that to spell them by the elementary sounds. A free use of sound-spelling possesses a double advantage: it makes the pupil familiar with the sounds represented by the letters, and it trains the organs of speech to give a clear and distinct utterance of each sound. Children who are thoroughly drilled in this manner have a more distinct articulation, a clearer pronunciation and read with more ease, fluency and elegance, than those who have not been thus drilled. The old practice of saying "spelling-lessons" from a spelling-book possesses but little advantage; it is far better to exercise the children to spell the words in their reading-lessons, carrying them at once from the Alphabet to reading. A child should not be permitted to attempt to read a sentence until it is able to pronounce every word in the sentence distinctly and promptly. Though the English language is not a phonetic language, in the sense that there is a printed character to represent every sound, nevertheless, the spelling of words and the pronouncing of syllables apart from words, assists the learner in arriving at a correct pronunciation of the word. Memory and the force of habit will enable pupils to pronounce correctly many words, that they have not before seen or heard. The ability to separate words into syllables with facility is of practical use in writing and printing, and is knowledge, therefore, worth obtaining. The spelling of simple words used in the literature of the first and second readers may be successfully taught by this method—that is, by rising from the sound of the elements to the pronunciation of the word.

The practice of requiring pupils to close their books and spell the words as pronounced by the teacher is, with children, more an act of memory than an operation of analysis. If a strange word is pronounced, that the children have not before seen, they will in all probability fail to spell it, unless it is so analogous to what is familiar, that they may readily guess the unknown by its similarity to the known. As soon as pupils are able to write with pencil or pen, this method of spelling should be abandoned.

SPELLING FROM PERCEPTION.

The second method of teaching spelling is here termed spelling from perception. A word is presented to the mind, either through the sense of hearing, or it is called up in a train of thought. The mind perceives the word, and this word is to be transferred into a written or printed form; by far the best practice, because it is logical, is to spell in writing.

From Dictation.—A profitable exercise in spelling is as follows: The class is arranged before the teacher, who reads from a book a few sentences, which each member of the class is required to write upon a slate, or, what is still better, upon paper, conveniently arranged for this purpose. After a sufficient number of words or sentences for the lesson shall have been written, the teacher may require some member of the class to spell the words in the first sentence; all who do not agree with the spelling of this pupil may signify it by raising a finger, and the teacher may require those, who dissent from the spelling, to spell the word as they have written it on the slate or paper. Other pupils may be required to read other sentences until the whole lesson has been gone over and corrected.

This exercise may be varied by taking the slips of paper upon which the members of the class have written and exchanging them, so that no pupil shall have in his hand his own writing; each may be required to state, after time has been given for inspection, whether all the words on the slip of paper in his hand are spelled correctly, and if any are incorrectly spelled, the pupil, who has detected the error, should be required to point it out and correct it. This exercise is similar to that afforded in the practice of proof-reading; here the reader is required to see that all words are correctly spelled. It also accustoms the pupils to detect, by sight, inaccuracies in spelling, and this is a valuable acquisition. It also gives the members of the class facility in writing; they will learn to write much more rapidly, in exercises like this, than they would in lessons of penmanship written out upon their desks. Spelling is rarely called into use orally, but it is of daily use, in writing, to vast numbers of those who are educated in the public schools. It is the experience of those who were apt spellers in school, and who stood at the head of spelling classes, and who were able in "spelling matches" to "spell down" all opponents, that this boasted attainment of school-day life was of little use in the active duties of later years. Spelling, to be taught practically, therefore, must be taught by the use of pencil and pen, and in that manner it becomes a daily exercise in almost every branch of learning. Exercises in arithmetic, in geography, in botany, in geology, in physiology, and especially in grammar and composition, are the very best drills in spelling, provided the teacher chooses to make them such. The knowledge of the correct use of capital letters and marks of punctuation is, by this method, acquired by practice, and will become fixed by force of habit long before the rules governing their uses are acquired from books.

Exercises in spelling, therefore, are reduced

to these uses: First, for purposes of drilling in the elementary sounds, and this should be continued throughout the study of elocution from the A-B-C class to the class in declamation; second, spelling for the purposes of business, which consists in writing words, should be taught by writing words, and these two methods may be varied so as to secure interest and efficiency.

GENERAL EXERCISES IN SPELLING.

Defective orthography is a matter of almost insuperable embarrassment to men and women, who are unable to spell the words of their language in ordinary use, and those, who do not learn to spell correctly in the public schools, rarely attain that accomplishment in after-life. Though one method may be better than another, no teacher should consider time as wasted, that is given to spelling exercises in almost any form. The whole school might be pleasantly entertained for a few minutes, frequently, by exercises in spelling; the more advanced pupils might be required to spell orally, or to write on their slates words of unusual orthography. The mistakes of some would make a lasting impression, so that they would be avoided by all in future. The younger pupils should be exercised in easier words, and even the children might print on their little slates a few simple words; the more advanced pupils should not be allowed to encroach upon the grounds of the little ones, or to criticise them too severely if they spell incorrectly. For purposes of spelling, the school might be divided into grand divisions; the division required to spell certain words could be announced before the words are given, and in this manner three or four words might be pronounced rapidly, and whilst the larger pupils were writing these, other words could be given to the smaller ones. Thus the teacher could pass from one division to another and pronounce words rapidly, so that in a few minutes the whole school would be at work and transfer them to their slates.

Another exercise could be introduced by conveniently dividing the school, as by placing those on one side of the main aisle against those on the other side, or the girls in opposition to the boys, so as to test the relative skill of the two divisions, and see which side would spell the largest proportion of a given number of words. This exercise could be conducted by requiring the pupils to write the words or to spell them orally. If, as is very often the case, a spirit of dullness settles down upon the school, so that neither pupils nor teacher know what to do with themselves, a pleasant relief may be introduced by a drill on the elementary sounds. Let the teacher write on the blackboard a few simple words, which the school may spell by sound in concert, the teacher leading and pointing to the letter that represents the sound to be given. This is a drill in which all can join, from the child studying the A B C to the most advanced classes, and all will be profited thereby. The teacher who varies these exercises so as to make them agreeable, and who succeeds in making of the boys and girls in his school correct spellers, will always be remembered with gratitude and pleasure by those who have enjoyed the advantages of his instruction.

PRONUNCIATION—ARTICULATION.

A correct pronunciation is even of more consequence than a correct orthography. Men talk more than they write, and therefore errors in pronunciation exhibit themselves more frequently than errors in orthography. It is impossible to converse in an edifying manner or to read well with habits of faulty pronunciation. To pronounce well requires the ability to articulate distinctly every element, and to utter plainly every syllable in a word. Distinct articulation requires a knowledge of the elementary sounds and the habit of giving to each a full and free utterance, and also of giving a distinct utterance to every syllable in a word. Pupils who are just passing from the learning of the Alphabet are usually taught pronunciation by spelling. The method pursued is to name the letters, pronounce the syllables and then pronounce the whole word. This is mainly for the purpose of enabling the pupil to determine what the word is. If, from the beginning, a distinct utterance of the sounds which the letters represent is required, there will be no difficulty as the pupil progresses in the study of elocution to maintain a correct pronunciation. In the utterance of the simplest and shortest words, therefore, the pupil must be required to produce every sound that enters into the composition of the word. If the teacher exercises due vigilance to detect and is prompt in calling attention to every error, there will be very little difficulty in leading his pupils into habits of correct pronunciation. This will lead to elegance in conversation and in reading. Defective pronunciation arises more from carelessness in articulation than from want of knowledge. The pupil knows perfectly well how to pronounce the words singing, judgment, education, yet by force of habit pronounces them as if written singin, judgemunt, edecation. The dropping of the *h* after the *w* in which, what, wheat and similar words is a very common defect, and this is done by force of habit. The work for the teacher, therefore, is to change habit, so that the same power which persistently enforces error may be made to enforce propriety. The pupil should be required to repeat frequently and rapidly, in a clear and distinct articulation, the words that he is in the habit of pronouncing defectively. All persons who are in the habit of carelessly and indistinctly pronouncing words may correct that habit by the power of repetition; this may be done at all hours in the day when the mind is not actively occupied in special duties, in walking to and from school, whilst retiring in the evening and rising in the morning; if the organs of speech are exercised in a mere whisper in the articulation of words that require correction in pronunciation, the defects will speedily disappear.

It is of little importance at what age or at what stage of progress the teacher receives pupils. If they have, by daily practice, either in the home-circle or under careless teaching in the public schools, acquired habits of defective pronunciation, it is his first duty to begin a practical system of training to correct the errors that his pupils have fallen into. What was said on the importance of a correct spelling is doubly emphasized on the subject of pronunciation.

The reward of the teacher will be immediate, for the most bungling and heavy-tongued among the pupils in the public school may, under a judicious system of training in articulation, be brought to a free use of his organs of speech in pronouncing the words of the English language.

In every school there will be found many pupils who have never been drilled in spelling by sound, who have never been required to exercise their organs of speech in distinct articulation, and to these the teacher should give the most careful attention, as many of them may be advanced in the course of studies, and will soon leave the public schools. It may be the last opportunity that such pupils will have for receiving proper instruction, that will enable them to correct these defects, which, if neglected in school, will follow them through life, causing them mortification in society, and standing as a barrier between them and cultivated people. Strangers, when first introduced to us, if they are accustomed to speak the same language that we do, are immediately judged from outward appearances. A defective pronunciation at once suggests ignorance and vulgarity. Frequently persons who are reasonably well educated and refined in manner have, through the bungling of schoolmasters, been permitted to grow up in habits of carelessness in articulation that ad here to them through life, and, therefore, these may often be erroneously classified, and that is an additional misfortune.

An arrangement of the letters of the Alphabet, which singly or in combinations represent the elementary sounds, convenient for drilling classes and schools, may be found on charts, in spelling-books and in readers very generally used in the public schools. The utterance of the vowel sounds is more readily acquired than the utterance of the sounds represented by those consonants usually denominated sub-vocals, or sub-vowels, or sub-tonics—that is, sounds between an open utterance, as in the case of vowel sounds, and a mere whisper, or breathing, as in the aspirates. A class may be drilled in the sub-vowel sounds somewhat in the following manner, viz.: Write on the blackboard the word BAT; require the class to pronounce it in concert, every pupil giving a full and complete utterance; remove the letter *t*, and require the class to pronounce the remaining part of the word, BA; remove the letter *a*, and require the class to give the sound represented by the letter *b*. This must be given with the lips closely pressed together, and it will require repeated efforts from all the members of the class to give a full utterance to this sound; yet it is precisely here that the chief distinction lies between a full, round, distinct pronunciation and a smothered, compressed and defective pronunciation. This order may be reversed. Write the word again on the board, BAT; require the class to pronounce it; remove the letter *b*, and require the class to pronounce the remaining AT; remove the letter *a*, and require the class to give the sound of the letter *t*. The class is now prepared to spell the word—not by naming the letters as is the usual mode, but by giving utterance to the elementary sounds. Other words, as dog, jug, bad, keg, lip, and the like, may be treated in the same manner as suggested above. The whole school should frequently be required to engage in an exercise like this, and all the pupils will derive great profit therefrom.

THE VOCAL ORGANS.

The vocal organs are those by which all sounds of the human voice are produced. They are the lungs, trachea, larynx, glottis and epiglottis.

The organs of articulation are those by which the sounds of the human voice are modified. They are the lips, teeth, tongue and palate.

A simple vowel is a sound produced without changing the position of the organs of articulation during the emission of breath.

A compound vowel is a sound produced by

changing the position of the organs of articulation during the emission of breath.

A teacher may illustrate the force of these definitions by uttering the sound of *a* in fate, which is a simple vowel, and the sound of *i* in fine, which is a compound vowel. Observe that while giving the *a* sound there is no motion of the organs of articulation, but in giving the *i* sound there is motion in these organs.

USING THE ORGANS OF ARTICULATION.

A Consonant is either a mere breathing or a sound interrupted by the organs of articulation.

The manner of using the organs of articulation gives rise to four divisions of consonants.

Consonants are labials, labio-dentals, lingua-dentals and lingua-gutturals.

Labials are articulations of the lips. They are represented by *p*, *b* and *m*.

Labio-dentals are articulations of the lower lip and the upper teeth. They are represented by *f* and *v*.

Lingua-dentals are articulations of the tongue and teeth, or gums. They are represented by *t*, *d*, *ch*, *j*, *s*, *z*, *sh*, *zh*, *th*, *l*, *n* and *r*.

Lingua-gutturals are articulations produced with the tongue rolled back against the palate. They are represented by *k*, *g* and *ng*.

Consonants may also be divided into sub-vocals and aspirates. A sub-vocal is a vocal sound suppressed by the organs of articulation. An aspirate is a whispering sound without vocality.

TABLE OF ELEMENTS.

The following is a simple form for a table of elementary sounds, which can be written upon a blackboard, or drawn upon a chart convenient for reference. It may also be used for concert exercises, in which the whole school may engage; or in class recitations.

ELEMENTARY SOUNDS REPRESENTED BY LETTERS OF THE ALPHABET.

VOWELS.

a,	ale,	ā.	e,	ell,	e.	o,	ox,	o.
a,	arm,	ä.	i,	ice,	ī.	u,	use,	ū,
a,	all,	a̤.	i,	it,	i.	u,	up,	u.
a,	at,	a.	o,	ode,	ō.	u,	full,	ṳ.
e,	eke,	ē.	o,	do,	ö.	ou,	out,	ou.

SUB-VOCALS.

b,	bid.	n,	nun.	s,	as.
d,	deed.	r,	rear.	z,	zest.
g,	gay.	v,	valve.	z,	azure.
j,	judge.	w,	woe.	ng,	song.
l,	lull.	y,	yell.	th,	that.
m,	mum.				

ASPIRATES.

p,	pop.	s,	siss.	th,	thin.
k,	kick.	sh,	ship.	h,	hat.
ch,	church.	t,	tat.	wh,	when.
f,	fife.				

COGNATES.

When two sounds can be produced without changing the position of the organs of articulation, they are called cognate sounds. Thus the sounds represented by *p* and *b* are cognates, also by *t* and *d*, *f* and *v*, *k* and *g*, *ch* and *j*, *s* and *z*, *sh* and *zh*, *th* and *th*.

The following suggestions will serve to guide the efforts of the teacher to overcome faulty and to establish correct articulation:

P and B.—The sound represented by *p* is formed by pressing the lips together before or after a vowel sound; the sound represented by *b* is produced by holding the lips in the same position and adding a sub-vocal utterance, so as not to emit breath through the nostrils.

T and d.—The sound represented by *t* is formed by pressing the tongue against the gums of the upper teeth; the sound represented by *d* is formed by holding the organs of articulation in the same position and uttering a sub-vocal sound. To complete the *t* sound it is necessary to drop the end of the tongue back from the teeth, but the *d* sound is completed with the organs in the position first assumed.

F and v.—The sound represented by *f* is formed by pressing the upper teeth gently upon the lower lip and emitting the breath; the sound represented by *v* is formed by holding the organs of articulation in the same position and uttering a sub-vocal sound.

K and g.—The sound represented by *k* is formed by pressing the middle part of the tongue firmly against the upper and back part of the palate; the sound represented by *g* is formed by keeping the organs of articulation in the same position and uttering a sub-vocal sound.

Ch and j.—The sound represented by *ch* is formed by pressing the tongue against the gums of the upper teeth and emitting the breath by slightly dropping the tongue; the sound represented by *j* is formed by holding the organs in this position and uttering a sub-vocal sound.

S and z.—*S* sometimes represents an aspirate and sometimes a sub-vocal sound; the latter is the same as that represented by *z*. The aspirate sound of *s* is formed by placing the tongue against the gums of the upper teeth so as to emit the breath over the tip of the tongue; the sound represented by *z* is formed by holding the organs of articulation in the same position and uttering a sub-vocal sound.

Sh and zh.—The sound represented by *sh* is formed by placing the sides of the tongue against the upper teeth and dropping the end of the tongue so as to nearly touch the gums of the lower teeth, and emitting the breath through the aperture thus formed; the sound represented by *zh* is formed by holding the organs of articulation in this position and uttering a sub-vocal sound.

Th and th.—The aspirate sound represented by *th* is formed by placing the tip of the tongue between the teeth and emitting the breath; the sub-vocal sound represented by *th* is formed by holding the organs in this position and giving a sub-vocal utterance.

These distinctions should be marked by teachers, and the pupils should be required to practice them until they are familiar. Defective or faulty pronunciations arise from a misplacing of the organs; the most effectual method, therefore, of correcting them, is by directing pupils in what position the organs of articulation must be placed in order to produce correct utterances. Errors most frequently occur in the use of cognate sounds which are interchanged, the one being substituted for the other by foreigners attempting to speak English. These defects will be removed by drilling in the cognate sounds as here indicated.

CHAPTER VII.

METHODS OF INSTRUCTION.—Continued.

READING.

METHODS of teaching reading are modified by the capacity of the pupils. Those passing from the spelling and pronouncing of words to reading, and until they are able to commit to memory and comprehend the simple rules of elocution, must be instructed orally. This is called the *First stage.*

The activity of Sense and Memory in childhood makes of children quick imitators. They, with little effort, almost exactly reproduce whatever impresses them forcibly, either in action or in speech. By the cultivation of this power they soon acquire skill in reading, and are thus prepared to enter upon the *Second stage* of learning to read. They may thus learn and observe certain simple and practical rules of pitch, force, time and inflection, and give attention to the cultivation of expression.

BEGINNING TO READ.

Reading is an art. It requires a knowledge of the alphabet, spelling and pronunciation. What has been taught or suggested in methods of teaching the alphabet, orthography and pronunciation must now be reduced to practice.

The first essential in good reading is distinct articulation and the prompt pronunciation of each word as it occurs in the composition. Articulation is the art of uttering distinctly the elementary sounds in syllables and words. If pupils have been thoroughly drilled in articulation, there will be little difficulty in leading them into habits of reading clearly and distinctly. A pupil should not be required to read a sentence until he is able to pronounce, at sight, every word in that sentence.

First of all, the difference between naming words and reading must be clearly pointed out. A child required to read without any previous instruction or direction on the subject will, in a forcible manner, pronounce one word after the other, from the beginning to the end of the sentence, and will consider that reading. In order to establish in the mind of the pupil the difference between this explosive style of pronouncing words, and reading, the teacher should write a short sentence on the blackboard, as, "James, bring me your hat." Let the teacher pronounce each of these words, not always in their regular order, and require the members of the class, one after the other, to do the same. Impress upon the minds of the pupils that reading is simply repeating from a book or paper, what some one else has said or written. Let the teacher say to his class, "Suppose you wish to ask James to bring his hat to you, and in order to do that you would use the words written on the blackboard, how would you pronounce these words?" It is probable that most of the class will read the sentence in an artificial style, in an elevated key and a drawling tone. This style may be corrected by telling one member of the class to look at the boy by his side and say to him, "Bring me your hat," just as if he wished him to go and get his hat for him. Practice this by varying it to meet the circumstances, until each member of the class reads the sentence on the board as he would speak it to a boy if he really asked for his hat. After several sentences have been treated in this way, the teacher may take up the class-book and select a short paragraph, divide it into sentences and the sentences into phrases; the smallest divisions should be read by all the members of the class, both individually and in concert. When the phrases in a sentence shall have been made familiar, some one in the class may read the whole sentence; every member of the class should read it, and the class should read it in concert. It is better to spend twenty minutes in learning how to read one sentence well, than to blunder over two or three pages without having established a definite idea of how to read any part of it. Reading as an art is first learned by imitation, and is afterward perfected by practice. In order to imitate, and also in order to practice, the pupil must have a model. Whenever, therefore, a single sentence or a short paragraph is so mastered by the class, that each member can read it correctly, that sentence or that paragraph will stand in the mind of the pupil as a model. An effort will thereafter be made to read other sentences and other paragraphs in the same style, and with the same facility, that the model passage is read.

THE FIRST READING LESSON.

In assigning to a class of beginners a reading lesson, the teacher should select a suitable paragraph, one that sets forth what is within the comprehension of the pupils; the pupils should then be instructed to study the lesson so as to be able to pronounce, rapidly and correctly, all the words in it. Before attempting to read, the class should be required to pronounce all of the more difficult words in the lesson; the teacher should then read the first sentence, repeating it two or three times, so as to enable the pupils to catch the exact style in which they are expected to repeat the words. Now let each member of the class read the sentence, the teacher pointing out defects in pronunciation, tone of voice, motion, force, pitch and inflection, not by introducing by name these qualities, or by attempting to teach rules for the governing of the voice, but by simply demonstrating by vocal illustrations to the pupils, that they read incorrectly, and by giving the correct rendering. The fact to be taught to a class just beginning to read is, that reading correctly involves more than the mere naming of the words in the passage in regular order. This accomplished, the pupils are prepared to put forth efforts to acquire the ability to do something more than to pronounce, correctly, words in sentences.

The teacher should impress upon the young pupils the idea that they are required simply to talk from the book. In a small reader, used in many of the schools, occurs this sentence: "Mother, William has taken his wheelbarrow into the garden." Bring the children to comprehend that this sentence requires precisely the same utterance, when found in the book, as it receives originally, when the little child ran to her mother to tell her that William had taken his wheelbarrow into the garden. Let each member of the class be required to state to the teacher how he or she would have pronounced this sentence, if using it originally. Bring out a natural and easy utterance, make that the model and carry it into the book, and the work is accomplished.

CORRECTING FAULTY STYLES.

Most teachers will find it necessary to do more than to establish habits of correct reading. They will be frequently called upon to break up habits of incorrect reading. This may best be done by drilling on a single sentence, short and within the comprehension of the pupil. Train those pupils who have been allowed to read in a sing-song style, with the voice pitched to a high key, to utter one short sentence correctly; print that upon a chart, or write it upon the blackboard, and allow it to stand as a model, and whenever such pupils fall back into their old habits point them to the model and require them to repeat it.

READING TOO MUCH.

Perhaps the greatest difficulty in the way of real progress in the art of reading is the pernicious practice of attempting to read too much. A class should be kept on a short piece of simple composition long enough to enable it to master the sense in every particular, and to bring out the full meaning in the reading. It is better to give weeks, or even months, to the thorough mastering of one short piece, than to listlessly read a book through in that time.

When a suitable piece shall have been selected, the teacher should make it a subject for conversation during the first recitation period. He should explain the meaning and sentiment of the composition in a style that is comprehended by the members of the class, and that will interest them in reading it over carefully. In the second recitation period, devoted to this piece, the teacher should require from the pupils an explanation of the thoughts contained in each paragraph and of the sentiment in the whole composition. After the whole theme has been made familiar to all, the class is ready to begin to read. The first paragraph should be read by each pupil, and should be re-read until every member of the class renders it correctly. The second paragraph may then be taken up and treated in a similar manner, and so likewise the other paragraphs, until the class is able to read each correctly; then each member of the class may be required to read the whole piece from beginning to end.

THE SECOND STAGE.

By the practice of reading from imitation, young pupils will very early attain that degree of advancement, at which the subject can be taken up and treated as one governed by principles that may be expressed in rules. From this point forward the method of instruction will be somewhat different. Hitherto the pupils have learned to read certain pieces by imitating the teacher, and by doing as nearly as possible what they were told to do. The first stage of learning to read ends when the purely oral methods of teaching are no longer required. Generally the teacher must be the judge of the proper time, at which to introduce rules of reading to his class. It will be better to postpone this change of method than to introduce it before the pupils are prepared to comprehend the rules, or to apply the principles of elocution set forth in them.

Before proceeding to the examination of more formal methods of teaching elocution, attention must be given to some general principles that should govern the teachers and authorities in the public schools. It is essential to keep in mind constantly the scope and limits of a public-school education. There is no branch of study pursued in these schools, which has been so warped and abused as the one now under consideration. A few traveling elocutionists have been able to turn the heads of many teachers, and to instill the idea, that the school-rooms throughout the country are the proper places wherein to teach elocution as a "high art." Men and women subject themselves to severe drills on a few pieces of humorous and pathetic composition, and then set themselves up as "elocutionists"; they visit normal schools, teachers' institutes, conventions and associations, where they "entertain" audiences by the recitation of their whole stock in trade. Under ordinary circumstances, considered as an entertainment, these exhibitions may not be objectionable, but, unfortunately, they are usually prefaced, or followed by lectures on the subject of reading, laboring to show that reading is nothing if not performed in the manner of these "elocutionists."

Elocution in its highest sense is a fine art. The ability to speak with force and elegance in original discourse, or in the rendering of the composition of others, is a very desirable acquisition. The objection made here is, that the teaching of this art, as presented by most professional elocutionists, is out of place in the public schools. For purposes of emphasis it is again repeated, that these schools are for the education of the millions. With reference to any study, therefore, or any exercise urged upon the consideration of the school authorities, the sole question to be determined is, whether it is desirable as a study, or exercise for the masses, who are educated in the public schools. With reference to the subject of reading, what is it that should be taught in these schools? Clearly this: the reading of colloquial and descriptive styles of composition with grace and fluency—that is, the children in the public schools should, by a judicious system of training, acquire the ability to read ordinary composition, such as is found in the Scriptures and other family literature, whether permanent, or ephemeral in its character, in such manner that they may understand it themselves, and that they who hear may comprehend the meaning of what is read. What is beyond this is technical, and no more belongs to the curriculum of the public schools, than the technical arts or sciences of other professions. A few simple rules, learned and applied, will give this ability to the pupil. The teacher should be critical in everything that is read, whether in the ordinary reading-book, or in recitations, in other studies, demanding that every sentence, whether standing alone or as part of a discourse, should be rendered correctly.

RULES.

The reading of every sentence involves PITCH, FORCE and TIME.

Pitch.—Pitch indicates the key, that is, the elevation or depression of voice in which a sentence is rendered. To enable all pupils to distinguish difference in pitch, require each member of the class to read a familiar sentence in an ordinary tone. Call that tone of voice for the pupil who reads the sentence, medium pitch; let the same pupil then read the same sentence in the highest possible key, in which he can give a distinct utterance; this call high pitch. The same pupil should be again required to read the same sentence in the lowest tone of voice, in which he can give a distinct utterance, and this may be called low pitch. Another pupil may be required to do the same thing, and may be able to read the sentence on a higher key, or on a lower key, or on both higher and lower keys, than the first. These terms, therefore, high pitch and low pitch, are relative, depending upon the register of the individual voice.

All ordinary composition is read in the medium pitch. Animated and exciting discourse is read in a high pitch. Grave and solemn composition is read in a low pitch. These general principles should be illustrated by the introduction of compositions thus differing in style, which should be read by the teacher and repeated by the pupils.

Force.—Force is a term applied to the power, or volume of voice used in uttering a sentence. Differences of force may be illustrated by persuing a method similar to that described on the subject of Pitch. There is a medium voice, a loud voice and a soft voice. The medium is the natural volume of voice, in which the pupil reads ordinary composition. Loud voice is the greatest volume of voice that the reader possesses. The soft voice is the most subdued volume of voice, in which the pupil can give utterance to a sentence.

The emotions of the heart are represented chiefly by the volume of voice used. When the heart is stirred with anger, the utterance is usually in a loud voice. When it is oppressed by grief, or moved in tender affections, the utterance is usually in a soft and mellow voice. The two extremes of Force and the medium should be illustrated in proper selections, to be read by the teacher and repeated by the class.

Force includes Articulation, Accent and Emphasis.

Articulation has already been treated of at considerable length under the several divisions of the alphabet, orthography and pronunciation, and also in the first stage of reading.

Accent.—Accent is also part of pronunciation. Habits of correct accentuation are acquired through the power of imitation. Rules of accent cannot, with propriety, be introduced to pupils who are learning to spell and to pronounce words. They learn accent, however, as it were, intuitively. Pupils readily accent words correctly that resemble those they have already learned to pronounce. Acquiring the ability to pronounce a word involves a practice of accentuation, but does not necessarily give a knowledge of the principles that govern accents. The rules of accent set forth in the readers are necessarily of little use. What is required from the teacher is promptness in correcting any false accentuation on the part of the pupils, and also to require the accent to be distinctly marked.

Emphasis.—Emphasis is the utterance of some word or words in a sentence with greater force, than those immediately preceding or following the emphasized part receive. Before the pupil can rightly determine what word or words should be marked by an increase of force, he must thoroughly comprehend the meaning conveyed in the sentence. A sentence is a collection of words expressing a thought. The leading idea is found in some one word or phrase in the sentence, and whatever precedes or follows this is used for the purpose of explaining or limiting. Emphasis is employed in giving utterance to bring out this leading idea, and to distinguish it from its surroundings. In the act of rendering a sentence, if the pupil misapplies the emphasis, the teacher should require him to explain the meaning—that is, to point out the leading idea in the sentence; after that has been done, there will be no difficulty in correctly placing the emphasis.

Time.—Time expresses the rapidity with which sentences are uttered. There is the ordinary or medium rate, which the habit of the individual establishes. There is a limit to the highest rapidity with which words can be uttered intelligibly. The other extreme is not so definitely marked. By slowness of time, therefore, is meant such deliberation of utterance as admits of considerable pause between the words.

It is desirable that all pupils should establish habits of reading with reasonable rapidity. When reading is a mental exercise, it is of great importance to the student to be able to read rapidly, whatever receives his attention, and much may be done in our public schools to cultivate habits of rapid reading. As an oral exercise, pupils should not be permitted to read with greater rapidity than will admit of a clear and distinct utterance of syllables, and of every word in the sentence.

In no case should a pupil be permitted to drawl out hesitatingly and indistinctly an exercise in reading. Promptness and distinctness should be required in the utterance of every sentence. If there is natural hesitation or diffidence, it may be overcome by frequent repetition of sentences or paragraphs, until they become so familiar that the teacher can force the time up to such a point of rapidity as would be desirable for the improvement of the pupil's style.

In treating of Pitch, Force and Time, only the well-marked distinctions have been noted; between medium and high and medium and low Pitch there are grades not well marked, however. The same observation applies to the graduations of Force and also of Time. It is more likely to produce confusion in the minds of the pupils, to attempt to mark these intermediate distinctions, than to result in any good.

When the fact is kept in view, that we are educating the masses of the people to do well, what they are likely to be called upon to do in their several spheres of life, the propriety of resting these distinctions as they are here made will be justified. If elocution is to be studied as an art for professional purposes, the application of time and effort, far beyond what is consistent with the public-school period, will give to the voice and passions, that training which will enable the reader to mark fine distinctions. These are required of professional elocutionists, but not of men and women who read in their homes for their own edification, or for the instruction of their families or friends.

Inflection.—By inflection is meant the modulations or slides of the voice from one key to another. There are three inflections, the Rising Inflection, the Falling Inflection and the Circumflex.

Rising Inflection is an upward slide of the voice, or the passing from a lower to a higher pitch.

Falling Inflection is a downward slide of the voice, or a passing from a higher to a lower pitch.

Circumflex is a combination of the Rising and Falling Inflections.

For general purposes these inflections may be applied as follows:

Direct questions—that is, such questions as may be answered by yes or no—are usually read in the Rising Inflection.

Indirect questions, or such as require a circumstantial answer, are usually read in a Falling Inflection.

Sarcasm and irony require the circumflex.

Composition expressing solemnity, majesty or awe is read without a change of voice—that is, in monotone.

Elocutionists are in the habit of forming numerous rules on the subject of Inflection, but those here given will serve as sufficient guides to the teachers and pupils in the public schools. The teacher, of course, is supposed to know something more. If in the course of reading, passages should occur requiring departure from these rules—that is, if exceptions to the general rules should arise—teachers should be able to point them out and give a reason for them. For example, a direct question, though read in the Rising Inflection, if repeated, takes the Falling Inflection.

Inflection may be presented to the pupils by writing a sentence on the blackboard and requiring the class to read it in the Rising Inflection and in the Falling Inflection. Examples in which circumflex may be applied should also be written on the board for the purpose of class drill.

Nearly all of the reading in common life is done in medium Pitch, medium Force and medium Time, but there is not this sameness in the use of Inflection. It is impossible to converse on any subject of interest for a space of five minutes without using, repeatedly, the Rising and Falling Inflections. Also in reading descriptive and colloquial styles, especially of the latter, Inflection is brought into constant and varied use.

Before a class is permitted to read a lesson, the questions of Pitch, Force and Time and of Inflection should be determined. It will be necessary to examine all parts of the selection critically, and the teacher should require the several members of the class to state the Inflection that may be properly applied to any questions that occur in the lesson.

When the subject of Inflection is first presented to a class, the teacher should select dialogues, or compositions in which frequent questions and answers occur, so that marked examples of Inflection may frequently arise for the determination and exercise of the pupils. A short dialogue covering two or three pages of a Reader, thoroughly mastered by a class, will do more to establish correct habits in the use of Force and Inflection, than all the rules and exceptions that have been invented by elocutionists. If it should require a daily drill, during a week or a month, to attain this result, the time may be considered as very profitably expended.

A few pieces well read, during one school-term, will do more to establish habits of correct reading, than the mumbling of all the selections found in a series of six or seven School Readers. The multiplication of books has also multiplied habits of careless reading and superficial instruction on the subject of elocution. There is no branch of common-school learning, in which quality and quantity are more widely separated than in the one now under consideration. It is absolutely necessary, in order to make good readers, that children shall be required to read well one selection before they are allowed to take up another. It may require days and weeks of study and of practice to become thoroughly familiar with the meaning of one simple composition, and the proper tones of voice to fully express that meaning. It is better, however, to continue the drill in one piece until every part of it is thoroughly mastered, until it is comprehended in letter, meaning and sentiment; it then is made part of the pupil's intellectual possessions; it is set up in the department of judgment as a standard; it becomes an ever-present model, up to which the possessor labors to bring every subsequent effort in elocution.

GENERAL OBSERVATIONS.

The principle, that a teacher should be educated in all branches of learning, that he attempts to teach, far beyond the requirements of his class, is so well established that, in the discussion of all topics, it is assumed as a fundamental condition. The rules given on the subject of elocution are thus deemed sufficiently practical for the purposes of a common-school education. Whether the teacher has attained great proficiency in the art of elocution, or whether he is simply what is understood by the phrase "a good reader," if he possesses the requisite culture the position he occupies demands, he will have clear ideas on the subject of style, posture, gesture and what is included in the single word, "Delivery."

First of all, the teacher should require the members of his class to rise before attempting to read. When necessary, he should give instructions to guide the pupil in assuming an easy posture—not a stiff, inflexible position—standing erect and firm. The book should be held in the left hand, and in a position that will enable the reader to distinctly see the composition which he is about to read. The reading should proceed with ease and fluency of utterance, and such modulation of voice as will be agreeable to the ear. If defects of voice are detected in any of the pupils, the teacher should give special attention, and, by repetition of suitable exercises, remove the defect if it is not organic.

Self-examination is of importance to both teachers and pupils. Ordinarily every man may be his own best critic; he has a standard of excellence of his own; he knows more of the circumstances, motives and purposes governing his action than any one else. The difficulty is that all men are more prone to criticise other people's action than their own. Before attempting to instruct a class how to read a selection, the teacher should read it himself, should criticise his own reading by carefully comparing the utterance with the sense, and after harmonizing the two as nearly as it is possible for him to do, he is prepared to meet his class. Such general instructions should be given to the individual members of the more advanced classes, as will enable them to practice self-examination and self-criticism in conversation and in reading.

Men frequently correct faulty pronunciation or clumsy utterances by making memorandums of these errors, as they occur, and then, by a severe and frequent drilling of the vocal organs when alone, overcome them. If a pupil is in the habit of reading exceedingly slow, instruct him to practice reading aloud when at home, reading as rapidly as possible, timing himself by the clock, so that by frequently repeating some familiar selection he may be enabled to increase the rate of speed at which he can distinctly utter the words. Attaining the ability to read one piece rapidly will effectually break the habit of slowness. Reading aloud to one's companions or when alone is a very valuable exercise, and all pupils should be encouraged to engage in it frequently. The ear readily detects errors or defects of voice which, by perseverance, may be overcome, but which, without the practice of reading aloud, would never be detected.

It very often occurs that far too much importance is attached to the reading of poetry. If composition in verse is of a high order, the sense is very often not so easily discovered by young pupils; the sentiment is not enjoyed, and thus the exercise is very often merely mechanical. More success will be achieved by practicing the reading of prose composition; it will be more satisfactory to the pupil. His attainments can be carried into immediate practice. Later in life, when the development of intellect and sensibility makes it possible to comprehend the productions of the best poets, the transfer of skill in prose reading will be easily made.

DECLAMATION.

For purposes of declamation a school should be so divided into convenient sections as to admit of an exercise by one of the divisions every week. A very general practice is to set apart half a day in a month, in which the whole school engages in exercises of declamation and composition. The practice here recommended is, that an hour each week be devoted to this subject. This will in no way interfere with the lessons of the younger children, who do not participate in this exercise. It will in no sense break in upon the regular order of the school, and will afford more frequent opportunity for instruction and criticism. Six or eight declamations might be delivered and as many compositions read within an hour, so as to allow time for brief and pointed instruction. The duty of the teacher, here, is to instruct his pupils, first, in the selection of suitable pieces to speak; second, in committing a piece to memory; third, in rehearsing the piece preparatory to speaking it on the stage.

Selecting Pieces.—Pupils should be instructed to select from good authors, whose writings abound in wholesome sentiment and correct teaching, to select short pieces, and to select composition which, in meaning, style and sentiment, is within their comprehension. If pupils are ambitious to speak long pieces, this ambition must not be gratified in the regular exercises of the school: on occasions of festivals, examinations or exhibitions these more extended efforts may be permitted, within certain limits; but for the regular drill exercises of the school, the teacher must insist that all pieces be short.

Preparation.—A piece that has been selected must be made the subject of careful study; the pupil should thoroughly comprehend the meaning of the composition before he attempts to commit it to memory. This may be accomplished by attentively reading it over and studying every part. After the meaning and sentiment are understood, the piece should be committed to memory; this must be done thoroughly, so that there will be no hesitation in reciting every word of it, from beginning to end. Thus the pupil may make the language, word for word, and the sentiment throughout the whole selection, his own.

Rehearsing.—Pupils should frequently repeat the pieces aloud, giving the proper utterance, in a clear and distinct articulation, to every syllable and word. When this can be done, they may be spoken from the platform to the school.

What the teacher should aim to establish for his pupils is the ability to come upon the stage with ease and naturalness of step, as if walking in a private room; to bow to the audience as he would to an acquaintance, gracefully; to stand in an easy, natural position; to avoid awkwardness and stiffness; to speak as if the words uttered were his own, and as if he wished to convince every person in the room, that he believed in the truth of every sentiment expressed in the composition. Calmness, deliberation, ease and grace of mien may be cultivated in these exercises, if the teacher will attentively mark the characteristics of each little speaker in his school, correcting the defects of the awkward, encouraging the efforts of the timid, repressing the bombast of the bold, stimulating the ambition of the indifferent. Thus he will, by proper attention and wise criticism, lift many of his pupils up to a desirable degree of proficiency in the art of declamation.

An elaborate system of elocution is out of place in the public schools, unless special classes are organized in the High Schools of towns and cities, for those who may desire to enter professions wherein oratory is especially useful. Teachers, therefore, are cautioned not to attempt too much in the way of declamation in mixed and graded schools. There is danger of encouraging and of cultivating a precocious development, and of exciting ambitions that will draw away the attention of pupils from their weightier studies in these exercises. They must be kept within proper limits; the instruction must be pointed and practical, and the criticisms must be mild and persuasive. The object of declamation in schools must not be lost sight of. It is to cultivate such confidence in the presence of audiences, that will enable men to speak with ease, force and clearness their sentiments, on subjects they may be called upon to discuss.

COMPOSITION.

Reading lessons may be used to illustrate the principles of composition writing. A composition, like a sentence, must have a subject. This subject is to be described, defined or explained. Descriptive composition is most natural and easy for young pupils. Describe what is known: a building, a tree, a farm, a cave, a lake, a factory, a grove. Relate what is known: the incidents of a journey actually made by the writer, what occurred at a meeting, at the post-office, in the village, in the church, in the school, in harvest-time, in winter, in summer. Pupils should avoid abstractions, select subjects for compositions from objects of sense, from things and scenes observed, beginning with the most simple and advancing to the more complex. The teacher should guide and encourage, even the smallest efforts, by gentle and suggestive criticisms.

CHAPTER VIII.

METHODS OF INSTRUCTION.—Continued.

"ARITHMETIC."

ARITHMETIC consists of explanations of principles and the application of those principles in operations of numerical combinations. The study of mathematics has two uses: *First*, to establish familiarity with numbers and to teach their application in the ordinary concerns of life; *second*, to discipline the mind by exercising it upon mathematical combinations. The scope of public schools limits the study of mathematics chiefly to the first of these uses. Mathematics cannot be studied solely for purposes of discipline in public schools, without excluding studies which are more useful to the masses, and which serve equally for purposes of discipline. This principle has been fully discussed in another part of this work.

Arithmetic, then, is studied in the public

schools for the purpose of establishing in the minds of the pupils a knowledge of the properties of numbers and their application in the concerns of life.

The fundamental rules of arithmetic are—Notation and Numeration, Addition, Subtraction, Multiplication and Division.

These fundamental rules find numerous and varied applications in arithmetical combinations. Combinations may be carried to an almost unlimited degree of complexity, so that it is an easy task to multiply examples in, and to increase the size and number of books on this subject. Arithmetic stands at the beginning of a course of mathematics.

NOTATION AND NUMERATION.

When a child enters school, he possesses some knowledge which has been obtained by observation. He distinguishes between one apple and two apples, perhaps between four apples and five apples. He may be able to count orally ten or twenty, or beyond this. Whatever the degree of knowledge, it is the duty of the teacher to ascertain the point where it ends, and precisely there is the place to begin instruction. In order to continue a familiar process of acquiring knowledge, teachers should direct the children to provide themselves with some small objects to be used in counting. Beans, corn or small pebbles will answer the purpose.

A class of beginners should be arranged about a table, each member with his counters before him. If all the members of the class are sufficiently advanced, the teacher may require them to count out twenty objects, moving one object as each number is named. The twenty objects counted may be separated by the pupils into sets of two each, and thus they will see how many twos there are in twenty. They may be separated into sets of ten each, and the pupils will see how many tens there are in twenty. This exercise may be varied to any extent that the teacher may deem proper or that the circumstances may require. By the use of the blackboard, the teacher may illustrate the operations performed by the pupils with their counters, and thus the children will learn to associate the figures on the board with the number of objects before them.

Pupils who studied the alphabet, spelling and pronunciation by the use of the slate and pencil will already be familiar with the forms and meaning of numerals, at least from one to nine. If they have not been thus drilled in the use of slate and pencil, they will require some special teaching, and the slate and pencil should at once be introduced. The children may be required to write upon their slates numbers representing objects exhibited by the teacher. The "arithmetical frame" may be employed to exhibit numbers and combinations of numbers, which the children may write upon their slates. A general class drill may also be carried on by the use of the blackboard; the teacher may rapidly draw a number of small circles, or make straight marks; he may remove some and draw others, questioning the class all the while, so that it will state correctly the number of strokes or circles on the board. As soon as the pupils are able to associate the written characters with the number of objects, they are prepared to engage regularly in written exercises in Notation and Numeration.

Schools should be supplied with a series of small charts containing, in large and distinct print, combinations of figures. The first chart should contain in one column all from one to nine, in other columns from ten to nineteen, from twenty to twenty-nine, etc., to ninety-nine. The second chart might contain numbers from one hundred to nine hundred, and from one thousand to nine thousand.

In the lessons upon the first chart the teacher will instruct the class, how any number of objects, from one to nine, may be represented by a single figure, and that all numbers over nine require more than one figure to express them. The pupils are supposed to have with them a supply of counters. They should first be required to count ten of these, and lay them in one place on the table, then to count another ten and lay it on the table. The teacher may illustrate on the blackboard that the figure one and a cipher represent ten, and that when two tens are brought together, instead of writing one ten twice, the figure two is substituted for the figure one, and that twenty is two tens. The meaning of thirty, forty, fifty, etc., may be explained in the same way, and this is deemed sufficient for the first exercise.

In the second lesson the teacher should explain how one ten and one unit make eleven. Here the little objects may again be employed. Ten are counted out, and one ten is written upon the blackboard, then a single object is taken and placed by the side of ten, and the teacher explains that the mode of writing this on the board is to remove the cipher and place a unit in the position the cipher occupied; then the one on the left represents one ten and the one on the right one unit; one ten and one unit are eleven units. Other numbers up to twenty may be constructed and explained in like manner. Twenty is two tens; two tens and one unit make twenty-one units, the cipher being again removed to make room for the unit. The counters in the hands of the pupils may be employed to illustrate the meaning of this combination. The same method is carried through to ninety-nine. One hundred is ten tens, and one hundred and one is ten tens and one unit; with slight variation the same devices employed to give pupils the idea of combinations below one hundred will be equally applicable in the construction of numbers above one hundred. These lessons in Notation and Numeration should be transferred by the pupils to their slates. The charts can be so placed that the pupils can copy from them while occupying their seats.

ADDITION.

Whilst teaching Notation and Numeration, operations of Addition and Subtraction will be carried on to such an extent that the pupils will be fully prepared to enter regularly upon the work of adding numbers. All arithmetics used in the public schools begin with simple combinations of numbers, so that in the first examples the sum of the column added is always less than nine. Pupils are supposed to possess such books. The teacher is required to explain the principles of Addition from the blackboard. The first idea to be impressed upon the pupil is that only things of the same kind can be added together. Thus, if in the class one boy has a bag of corn and another a number of pebbles to be used as counters, five pebbles and four grains of corn will not make nine pebbles or nine grains of corn. This illustration is useful to explain that five units and four tens cannot be added so as to make nine tens or nine units. Units must be added to units and tens must be added to tens. If Notation and Numeration have been thoroughly taught, the pupils understand that when two figures are placed side by side the left-hand figure is tens, and, therefore, if in adding the column the sum is expressed in two figures, the figure on the right hand is units and that on the left is tens, and as the column added is units and the next on the left is tens, the number representing tens in the sum must be added to the column of tens. This is the whole subject. The lesson must be enforced by a variety of illustrations sufficient to impress it upon the mind of the pupil.

SUBTRACTION.

No principles are employed in the operations of Subtraction that are not taught in the operations of Addition. The question for the pupil to settle is, how many units must be added to the subtrahend to make it equal to the minuend. This, in all examples, in which each figure in the minuend is larger than the one immediately under it, is all that the pupil is required to determine; but when some figure in the minuend is smaller than the one standing immediately under it, the operation of taking one unit from the next figure on the left and adding it to the figure that is too small, thereby increasing it by ten, must be explained. This is a reversal of the operation learned in Addition. The fact that the figure standing on the left represents ten times as much as the same figure would if standing on the right, is again called up. When the figure on the left is carried over to the column on the right, it loses none of its value; therefore the figure in the subtrahend is subtracted from the figure in the minuend increased by ten units. When the next figure in the subtrahend is to be taken from the figure above it, the fact, that the upper figure has been diminished by taking one from it to add to the figure on the right, must be recognized—that is, the figure is now treated as representing units, and as one unit was borrowed from it, which made ten when it was added, it is now treated as diminished by the subtraction of one. This may be illustrated, if necessary, by the use of the pupil's counters. If the minuend consists of three tens and two units, and the subtrahend of one ten and four units, these numbers may be counted out in beans; if from three tens, which may consist of three sets of beans of ten each, one set is removed, and its ten units are added to the two units, from which the pupil is required to subtract four units, there will be ten units and two units, which make twelve units, and by taking away four beans it is demonstrated that eight beans, or units, remain. Now, in the place where there had been three sets of tens only two sets remain, and from these two sets of ten beans each one ten is to be subtracted, which leaves one ten; one ten and eight units is therefore written as the answer.

MULTIPLICATION.

The operations in Multiplication proceed on exactly the same principles as those in Addition; instead of adding one number to another, it is now required to add a number to itself a given number of times; the multiplicand is to be added to itself as many times, less one, as there are units in the multiplier. The pupils should be taught to construct a multiplication-table by the aid of their counters. Thus a boy with a quantity of beans may ascertain for himself how many two times one are, how many two times two are, how many two times three are, and how many two times four are; by the same process, how many five times two are, how many five times seven are. The teacher should direct the pupils to carry on these operations in regular order, to rule their slates properly, and to write upon them their conclusions; in this manner they will be able to construct a complete multiplication-table, from two times one to twelve times twelve. When this table shall have been completed and approved by the teacher, it may be copied by the pupils upon paper. Thus all may be taught how the multiplication-table is constructed. Pupils will more readily and eagerly commit to memory what they have themselves produced, and will surprise their parents and friends by communicating the fact to them that they have made a multiplication-table just like the one in the book. The application of this table is the end of the exercises in Multiplication.

DIVISION.

Operations in Division are also similar to those taught in Addition. The pupils are required to ascertain how many times the divisor must be added to itself in order to make it equal to the dividend, and the number that indicates how many times this must be done is called the quotient. Or, to employ the training obtained in the construction and use of the multiplication-table, the question is, how many times must the divisor be multiplied in order to equal the dividend? When there are several figures in the dividend, and the divisor is not contained a number of times into any one of these without a remainder, how that remainder is added as tens to the next figure on the right as units must be explained. This may be done, if it is deemed necessary, by the use of the counters.

These are called the fundamental rules of arithmetic. Pupils should be drilled in solving problems involving these rules, unembarrassed by any other principles or combinations, until they are thoroughly familiar with them. Teachers should make it an invariable practice not to allow pupils to advance beyond the examples under these rules until this groundwork is thoroughly performed. All subsequent operations in numbers consist simply in the variations of the combinations and applications of these rules. Facility in their use, therefore, will be of advantage throughout the study of mathematics.

DENOMINATE NUMBERS.

The school arithmetics in common use usually introduce, immediately after the fundamental rules, tables of currency, weights and measures, and the examples presented for solution employ numbers denoting currency value, weight and measure. It may be proper, at this point, to introduce the subject of the currency of the United States and the weights and measures employed in the ordinary business transactions of the country. All other tables should be deferred to the closing portion of the common-school arithmetic. What is to be introduced here, then, is a table of the currency of the United States, a table of avoirdupois weights, a table of dry and a table of liquid measure, and tables of linear measurements; tables of foreign currency, apothecaries' weight and troy weight, and such other technicalities as are sometimes introduced in arithmetics, should not be presented to the pupil at this early stage of his progress. In view of the efforts now being made by the leading nations of the world to reduce to one system the weights and measures used in mercantile transactions, the metric system, which seems to meet with general favor and is the one most likely to be adopted, may properly find place in the arithmetic, nearer the end of the book, however, than the subject now under consideration. It will require no special skill on the part of the teacher to introduce these denominate numbers, inasmuch as at the beginning of the instruction in arithmetic denominate numbers were first used in the case of the beans, corn and pebbles brought to school by the children.

Those absurdities in modern arithmetics invented in early times, when it was useful to know how to reduce a given sum from one currency to another, or from a given weight to another, which are now of no possible use, should be excluded from common-school arithmetics, or when found there should be passed over without notice.

FRACTIONS.

One of the most interesting and delightful portions of arithmetic is the subject of fractions when it is logically presented and clearly demonstrated in all. its principles. When it is bunglingly presented, without proper explanations or demonstration, it is one of the most difficult, embarrassing, tedious and discouraging passages in the study of mathematics. In presenting the subject of fractions to a class, the teacher should occupy the time of the first recitation in demonstrating, by numerous devices, so that each member of the class will clearly comprehend, first, what a fraction is; secondly, what the numerator is; third, what the denominator is; fourth, the relations of the numerator and denominator to the unit; and fifth, the relations of the numerator and denominator to each other.

What is a Fraction?—The definition tells us a fraction is part of a unit. The teacher may have on his desk an apple and a knife; he may divide the apple into two equal parts, and say to his class, "This apple is a unit; if I divide it into two equal parts, one of these parts is called one-half; if I divide one of these halves into two equal parts, one of these parts will be one-fourth of a unit, or apple." Using the blackboard, the teacher may write $\frac{1}{2}$, which represents a part of the unit, and is therefore a fraction. He may write $\frac{1}{4}$, which represents a part of a unit, and is therefore a fraction; the subdivision of the unit may be carried forward by dividing the parts of the apple as far as practicable, carrying the notation on the blackboard parallel with the division of the object. Thus the idea of a fraction will be impressed upon the minds of the pupils.

The Numerator and Denominator.—Now let the teacher take up two parts of the divided apple, two-fourths, if they remain, or if not, a second apple may be divided for this purpose; going to the blackboard, he will illustrate the manner of writing $\frac{2}{4}$, the manner of writing $\frac{3}{4}$, the manner of writing $\frac{2}{8}$ and $\frac{3}{8}$, enforcing the idea now, that the figure below the line, called the denominator, shows into how many parts the unit has been divided, and the upper figure, which is called the numerator, shows how many of these parts of the unit are expressed in the fraction. Thus, when the apple is divided into two equal parts, the denominator is 2; when it is divided into four equal parts, the denominator is 4; when it is divided into eight equal parts, the denominator is 8. When one of these parts, is to be represented, the figure 1 is used as a numerator, as, $\frac{1}{2}$, $\frac{1}{4}$, $\frac{1}{8}$; when two of these parts are to be expressed, the numerator is 2, as, $\frac{2}{2}$, $\frac{2}{4}$, $\frac{2}{8}$.

The denominator also indicates the size of the parts. In the fractions $\frac{1}{2}$, $\frac{3}{4}$, $\frac{5}{8}$, the denominator 2 shows that the unit is divided into two equal parts, and that, therefore, one of the parts is half of the unit; the denominator 4 shows that the unit is divided into four equal parts, and, therefore, one of these parts is a fourth of the unit. It is, therefore, seen that $\frac{1}{2}$ is larger than $\frac{1}{4}$, and that $\frac{1}{8}$ is smaller than $\frac{1}{4}$, and still smaller than $\frac{1}{2}$.

The relation of the Numerator and Denominator to the Unit.—It has been demonstrated that the denominator of a fraction shows the number of parts into which the unit is divided, and also the size of the parts; that the numerator represents the number of these parts included in the fraction; therefore, as the denominator increases, the size of the parts of the unit diminishes, and hence the fraction diminishes. The reverse of this is true of the numerator, as the numerator represents the number of parts of the unit that are expressed by the fraction; the increase of the numerator increases the number of parts, the size of which remains the same, that are to be included in the fraction, and, therefore, the increase of the numerator increases the value of the fraction. By increasing the fraction is meant bringing the value or size of the part it expresses more nearly to that of the unit. That is, the parts or the sum of the parts are made more nearly equal to the whole.

This lesson should be illustrated by dividing and sub-dividing an apple or other convenient object, and combining the parts so as to enforce it upon the mind of the pupil, and thus the principle is brought out that the value of a fraction is increased by increasing the numerator, or by decreasing the denominator, and that the value of a fraction is decreased by diminishing the numerator or increasing the denominator.

The relation of Numerator and Denominator to each other.—When a unit has been divided into a number of parts, and several of these parts are to be represented, it will frequently occur that both numerator and denominator may be diminished without affecting the value of the fraction. Thus, suppose the unit has been divided into eight equal parts, and it is proposed to represent six of these parts; this will require the form $\frac{6}{8}$, but $\frac{6}{8}$ is the same in value as $\frac{3}{4}$. For practical purposes it is convenient to express fractions in the lowest possible terms. Now it has already been explained that diminishing the numerator decreases the value of the fraction, and diminishing the denominator increases the value of the fraction in the same ratio. If, therefore, the numerator 6 be divided by 2, and the denominator 8 be divided by 2, the result will be $\frac{3}{4}$; and thus the principle is deduced that multiplying or dividing both the numerator and denominator by the same number will not alter the value of the fraction.

OPERATIONS IN FRACTIONS.

With a thorough knowledge of the principles just explained, pupils will experience but little difficulty in performing operations in fractions.

Reduction of Fractions.—In the very beginning of the study of arithmetic, pupils are taught that only such numbers as represent the same things can be added to each other. This principle applies throughout all arithmetical processes. The denominator of a fraction shows the number of parts into which the unit has been divided. In attempting to add or subtract fractions, it is necessary first to bring them to the same denomination, thus, $\frac{3}{4}$ and $\frac{3}{8}$, if added to each other, would not make fourths, or eighths, or twelfths; they must be brought to the same denomination before they can be added. Applying the principle that the value of the fraction is not changed by multiplying the numerator and denominator by the same number, it is seen that $\frac{3}{4}$ may be reduced to $\frac{6}{8}$, and the problem will then be to add $\frac{6}{8}$ to $\frac{3}{8}$, which give $\frac{9}{8}$.

If the problem had been one of subtraction, the same process of reduction would have been necessary, $\frac{3}{8}$ from $\frac{6}{8}$ would leave $\frac{3}{8}$. The only element, therefore, entering into addition and subtraction of fractions, which is not employed in adding and subtracting units, is the element of the reduction to the same denomination: $\frac{3}{8}$ are added to $\frac{6}{8}$ in the same way that three beans are added to six beans; in one case the sum is nine-eighths, and, in the other, nine beans.

Multiplication of Fractions.—If a fraction is to be multiplied by a whole number, it is required to increase the fraction as many times as there are units in the whole number by which it is to be multiplied. The pupil knows already that a fraction may be increased by multiplying the numerator or by dividing the denominator. If $\frac{1}{4}$ is to be multiplied by 2, this may be accomplished either by multiplying the numerator 1 and writing the result thus, $\frac{2}{4}$, or by dividing the denominator by 2 and writing the result thus, $\frac{1}{2}$. In order to express the fraction in its lowest terms, the latter process is preferable in all cases where the denominator is divisible without a remainder by the multiplier.

If it is required to multiply a whole number by a fraction, as, to multiply 6 by $\frac{3}{4}$, the teacher should explain that the process will be the multiplication of 6 by $\frac{1}{4}$ of 3; therefore, if 6 be multiplied by the numerator 3, the product will be four times too large, because the multiplier given is not 3, but only $\frac{1}{4}$ of 3. It must therefore be reduced by dividing it by 4. Pupils should be required to perform solutions of such examples, and to state the reason for each step in the process.

If it is required to multiply a fraction by a fraction, it is necessary to state to the class that the multiplicand is to be multiplied by such part of the numerator of the multiplier as is expressed by the denominator of the multiplier; thus, if $\frac{3}{4}$ is to be multiplied by $\frac{2}{5}$, the requirement is to multiply $\frac{3}{4}$ by $\frac{1}{5}$ of 2. If $\frac{3}{4}$ be multiplied by 2, which may be done by multiplying the numerator by 2, giving $\frac{6}{4}$, the product is as many times too large as there are units in the denominator of the multiplier—that is, in this case it is five times too large. It must, therefore, be reduced to that extent. This can be accomplished by dividing the product by five. The fraction may be divided by multiplying the denominator.

Doing this, the result is $\frac{6}{20}$ or $\frac{3}{10}$. This rule is therefore deduced, that a fraction is multiplied by a fraction by multiplying the numerators together for a new numerator and the denominators together for a new denominator. The product should always be reduced to its lowest terms.

Division of Fractions.—The teacher should demonstrate on the blackboard the processes in the division of fractions. To divide a fraction by a whole number, the purpose is to decrease the fraction as many times, less one, as there are units in the divisor. It has been demonstrated that a fraction may be decreased by diminishing the numerator or by increasing the denominator. This has already been sufficiently explained.

To divide a whole number by a fraction, it is required to decrease the whole number as many times, less one, as there are units in a divisor, which itself stands in the relation of a dividend to another divisor—that is, if 6 is to be divided by $\frac{3}{5}$, it is required to divide 6 by $\frac{1}{5}$ of 3. If, therefore, 6 is divided by 3, the quotient 2 is five times too small, because the divisor used is that many times too large; it must, therefore, be multiplied by 5, the result being 10.

When a fraction is to be divided by a fraction, the requirement is the same as when a whole number is to be divided by a fraction. But the application of the principle involves also the division of a fraction, and this fraction is to be divided by such part of the numerator of the divisor as is expressed by the denominator. If $\frac{3}{4}$ is to be divided by $\frac{2}{5}$, it is required to divide $\frac{3}{4}$ by $\frac{1}{5}$ of 2; $\frac{3}{4}$ may be divided by 2 by multiplying the denominator by that number, which gives $\frac{3}{8}$, but inasmuch as it is required to divide $\frac{3}{4}$ by only $\frac{1}{5}$ of 2, the quotient is necessarily five times too small, and must, therefore, be increased to that extent. A fraction is increased by multiplying the numerator; by applying this principle the result is $\frac{15}{8}$. Thus the rule is deduced, that a fraction is divided by a fraction by multiplying the denominator of the dividend by the numerator of the divisor, and by multiplying the numerator of the dividend by the denominator of the divisor. Of course, in all cases in which the numerator and denominator of the dividend are divisible, without remainder, by the numerator and denominator of the divisor, that is the direct process.

PROPORTION.

The definitions of Ratio and Proportion, usually found in the school arithmetics, are sufficiently accurate for the purposes of the following explanation. The teacher is supposed to be familiar with these definitions. In presenting the subject to his class, he proceeds to deduce, by processes within the comprehension of the pupils, the principles of proportion, and the rules by which proportions are constructed and solved. He writes upon the blackboard two numbers, as 6 and 3; by division, 3 is contained in 6 twice. This relation between 6 and 3 is called ratio, and is expressed by the figure 2. If the numbers 8 and 4 are written upon the board, the same relation or ratio will be found to exist between them, and may also be expressed by the figure 2. That is, the relation between 6 and 3 is the same as between 8 and 4. The ratios are equal. The teacher may explain, that when two numbers are placed in such relation to each other, the first is called the antecedent and the second the consequent; the two terms when taken together are called a couplet. Ratios exist only between numbers of the same kind, or between abstract numbers. It would not be proper to say that the ratio between 6 apples and 3 turnips is the same as between 8 boys and 4 girls. If the numbers are denominate numbers, the antecedent and consequent of a couplet must be of the same denomination.

When ratios are equal, this fact is usually expressed by placing them opposite to each other, thus, 6 : 3 :: 8 : 4, and this formula expresses the equality of ratios—that is, the relation of 6 to 3 is equal to the relation of 8 to 4. When thus written, the one on the left is called the first couplet, and that on the right the second couplet, and the formula thus expressed is called a proportion. A proportion, therefore, is an equality of ratios. The first and the fourth terms are called the extremes, and the second and third the means, of the proportion. These terms in every proportion sustain such a relation to each other, that the product of the means is always equal to the product of the extremes. If, therefore, one of the means or one of the extremes of a proportion is wanting, it can be found by dividing the product of the extremes by the given mean, or, in the other case, by dividing the product of the means by the given extreme.

All this should be fully and clearly demonstrated by the teacher on the blackboard. The members of the class should be continually questioned, both to direct their attention and to assure the teacher, that they comprehend his explanations. The principles should then be summed up succinctly:

Ratio is the relation with respect to value that one of two similar numbers bears to the other.

Proportion is an equality of ratios.

The members of a proportion are called

couplets; both terms of the couplet must be of the same denomination.

The relation between the first and second terms of a proportion must be the same as the relation between the third and fourth terms.

The product of the means is equal to the product of the extremes.

A missing extreme may be found by dividing the product of the means by the given extreme.

A mean may be found by dividing the product of the extreme by the given mean.

With these principles fully comprehended, the class is prepared to advance to the consideration of problems involving proportions. Take an example: If 12 eggs cost 36 cents, what will 9 eggs cost? This, or a similar problem, the teacher may announce to his class and proceed to construct from it a proportion. It is not at all necessary to consider the required term as the fourth term of the proportion, though for uniformity in practice, this established custom may be adopted. In the problem here given the number to be found is the price of 9 eggs; this will be expressed in cents. It is, therefore, evident that the fourth term will be in the denomination of cents; the third term must be of the same denomination, according to the principles already demonstrated. The only number in the problem of this denomination is 36, the price of 12 eggs; 36 must, therefore, be written as the third term of the proportion. The fourth term, when found, will be the price of 9 eggs; the third term is the price of 12 eggs, and is, therefore, larger than the fourth will be; when the second couplet is complete, therefore, the antecedent will be larger than the consequent. The principles of a proportion require, that the ratio in the first couplet shall be the same as that in the second; therefore in the first, the antecedent must be larger than the consequent. Of the two remaining terms, 12 eggs and 9 eggs, 12 is the larger, and must be written as the antecedent, and 9 as the consequent, of the first couplet; the proportion stands thus, 12 : 9 :: 36 : —. Here is a proportion incomplete by the absence of one extreme. By the principles already enunciated, this is found by multiplying the means and dividing their product by the given extreme, $36 \times 9 \div 12 = 27$, and the complete proportion is, 12 : 9 :: 36 : 27.

This whole subject may be clearly presented to a class at one recitation of twenty minutes' duration. Teachers should immediately give other examples, or direct the pupils to open their books to the first examples given under the rule, and proceed to construct proportions by the application of these principles. The pupils should be required to run through the process of reasoning, rapidly, stating how the proportion in a given problem shall be constructed and how it shall be solved; in most cases the result may be announced without the necessity of transferring the numbers to a slate or blackboard. This introduces a proper application of mental arithmetic.

This method of presenting and explaining the subject of proportion is infinitely preferable, and is much more salutary in its effects upon the minds of the pupils, than the old practice of memorizing the definitions and rules, which are afterward to be applied, without any very definite idea of their meaning.

A Lesson in Proportion.—Let it be supposed that a class in arithmetic is engaged in the solution of problems involving the principles of proportion, that yesterday, ten problems were solved and demonstrated upon the blackboard by the class, and that to-day, an equal number of problems is to be recited. The proper mode of conducting this recitation is as follows: The most difficult problems in the lesson are assigned to pupils, one to each, who are required to proceed to the blackboard and to write out the solutions complete; whilst this is being done, the remaining members of the class are directed to open their books at the lesson of yesterday; the teacher designates some member of the class, who is required to proceed to solve, mentally, the first problem in yesterday's lesson—that is, to relate, without the use of visible signs, the processes involved in the solution. Another member of the class solves the second problem in a similar manner, and thus the lesson of yesterday is reviewed through the operation of mental solutions, performed by those members of the class, who are not required to solve problems on the blackboard. Those problems in to-day's lesson, which are deemed not sufficiently intricate to require solutions upon the blackboard, may also be solved mentally by members of the class. As soon as any one of the pupils at the blackboard shall signify that the problem assigned has been solved, the progress of the mental solutions in the class is suspended, while the pupil, with a suitable pointer in his hand, proceeds to explain to teacher and class the processes of the solution on the board. In this manner the whole class is actively employed during the whole time of the recitation; there is an exercise in written arithmetic and an exercise in mental arithmetic every day. The difficult problems are solved and demonstrated by members of the class, who thus exercise their faculties in performing mathematical operations, and in explaining to others, in what manner these operations are carried on and the final result obtained. This is an exhibition of knowledge possessed, and an exercise in the art of explaining to others what they should know. The solution of all problems in arithmetic mentally—by which is meant carrying on the processes in the mind without giving written expression—trains the mind in habits of definite and rapid thought, and accustoms the pupil to the use of language called up instantly to give expression to the thoughts evolved by mental operations. This is the best preparation for the scenes and duties of active life. It converts written exercises into mental exercises; it employs all the time actively, so that every moment is converted to good purposes and makes "mental arithmetic," as a distinct study, altogether unnecessary.

Sufficient has now been said on the subject of teaching arithmetic to establish the general principles involved in the method here set forth. The teacher should in every case lead his class, demonstrate principles and deduce rules, so that pupils will be able to see how, from the combinations of principles, rules and processes are evolved; they will follow the teacher through every demonstration, and in many cases mentally reach the result before the teacher has evolved it on the blackboard, or has announced it to his class The immediate application of the rules thus deduced is easy and agreeable, and if, throughout the study of arithmetic, the practice in mental solutions in review lessons is made a daily exercise, the principles will be so fully impressed upon the minds that pupils will not be required to drag this study along through the whole period of school-life. When a class has thus gone through arithmetic, all the members of it will have a clear comprehension of the subject, and will have experienced the lively satisfaction, that always results from a consciousness of knowledge possessed. They will, at the end of the term, lay aside the class-book with the agreeable confidence that they have thoroughly mastered all that is in it. Such a class may advance to the study of natural philosophy, physiology, botany or other sciences wherein the fundamental principles of arithmetic will be applied, and thus frequently passed under review. The process of mental discipline will be carried on so much more vigorously, through labors in these new fields of research, that it is an indignity to an active intelligence to force, on the plea of discipline, a retracing of studies in arithmetic. To exercise, for years, pupils thus thoroughly drilled in the ground-work, in the application of simple rules in intricate processes, under the mistaken notion that only thus, in public schools, can needful mental culture be obtained, would be a misfortune, a blunder, if not a crime.

The study of arithmetic in mixed schools should not be extended beyond the study of Fractions, Proportion, and Percentage, including Interest and Discount, illustrations of business forms used in the making up and adjusting of accounts, and superficial measurements as employed for ordinary business uses. This contemplates and embraces a course in Bookkeeping, in which the essential principles, and the practical system of entries and transfers, used in the actual operations of the counting-house, will be taught. What is beyond this is technical, and belongs to special branches of learning to be pursued by those, who wish to qualify themselves for special vocations, but is not at all of concern to the great masses, who are educated for the common affairs of life in public schools. Mathematical intricacies are superseded for purposes of discipline, and are therefore altogether ruled out of the public-school curriculum as useless.

CHAPTER IX.

METHODS OF INSTRUCTION.—Continued.

GEOGRAPHY.

THE method of teaching Geography which is here commended, presupposes that the teacher will not merely assign lessons, ask questions and hear answers, but that he will *teach* Geography to the class.

Geography, as applied to the study in public schools, is a description of the earth's surface, the surrounding atmosphere, the people and other living creatures that inhabit the earth, its soil and productions, together with such modifications as have been effected by man, including political divisions, political institutions, public improvements, etc. A mass of facts is to be presented in some methodical order to young pupils. The method usually adopted in most schools is, to place the Geography and atlas of some author in the hands of pupils, assign a lesson, require them to study it and appoint a time for recitation. The recitation is conducted by the teacher, who takes up the book and asks the questions printed in small type, and requires the pupils to repeat the answer as printed in large type. In this manner the preliminary definitions, the astronomical part, the political divisions, the races of men and a scrap of physical Geography are disposed of. The study of the grand divisions, of political divisions, including public improvements, products, governments and religions, are treated in the same superficial manner. This pernicious system was built up and is now fostered by the authors of Geographies, most of whom are disposed to follow a stereotyped form of compilation. Thus, one common-school Geography differs from another chiefly in the phraseology of questions and answers, illustrations and maps.

The natural method of presenting Geography to a class of beginners is found in the nature of the subject to be studied. First, knowledge of the general appearance of the earth's surface is to be acquired; secondly, the operations of nature proceeding on a large scale upon the earth's surface, such as the changes of seasons, currents of air and water, and the distribution of people and other living creatures; thirdly, the changes produced by man upon the earth's surface, such as the building of cities and towns, construction of highways, as canals, railroads and turnpikes, the founding of empires, of governments, commerce, and the like. Each of these general divisions comprises several subdivisions; these will be indicated in the discussion of the general divisions.

The Earth's Surface.—The first lessons in Geography should be confined to descriptions of the earth's surface. The proper place to begin is at the door of the schoolhouse. In the immediate vicinity of every school, there may be found some feature that may be taken as the beginning for a lesson. There may be a stream of water, a creek or river, that passes through a valley or between mountains. Here there are characteristics to be described. Tracing the course of the stream toward its source, the teacher may describe the general appearance of the country on both sides of it, stating how far the source is from the point of observation and what streams are combined to produce that which flows by the schoolhouse. He may pursue the course of the stream downward and describe the scenery on both of its banks, state what other rivers or streams flow into it, and where it empties its ever-flowing current into some other stream, into some lake, sea, bay, gulf or ocean. Possibly a spring, bubbling up from the earth near the schoolhouse, may be a most convenient starting-point for a lesson. Whence comes this water that issues from the earth and flows down upon the slopes on its surface? Here the rising of vapors, the forming of clouds, the falling of rain, may be described, as the processes by which water is taken up from and returned to the earth. Then the course of the rivulet flowing from the spring may be followed until it joins itself to some other stream. The stream of the combined rivulets may be traced until it unites with some river, and thence finds its way to the ocean.

The schoolhouse may be among mountains or it may be on a plain; it may be in country or it may be in city; but wherever it is, let the description of the earth's surface begin there, and spread out in all directions, and combine all features, until the idea of the pupil embraces the surface of the whole earth. These descriptions, it is true, will not be exhaustive. They will not be technical. In a scientific sense they may not be complete, but for the purpose of teaching Geography to a class of beginners, they may be complete.

This will be accomplished solely by oral instruction. No books are used; none are required. The idea of a valley, of a mountain, of a plain, of a river, of a lake, of a sea and ocean, the idea of great water-currents and great air-currents, of clouds, of rain, of canals, of railroads, of turnpikes, of villages, of cities, counties, townships, school districts, will be grasped more readily by this method than by efforts to communicate them through formal lessons framed by bookmakers.

If the class is one of small children, the teacher may use the blackboard in describing water-courses, mountains and plains, in noting sites of cities, in representing canals, railroads and turnpikes, so that pupils will become accustomed to associate the sketches on the board with the features or objects they are designed to represent, and they will thus be better prepared to enter upon the study of Geography by the use of books and maps. The average capacity of the class and the fertility of the region of country in distinguishing features of surface, will enable the teacher to determine the extent to which these oral exercises shall be carried. That teacher, who will put forth efforts to frame such lessons for his classes during the first week, or even two weeks, of their study of Geography, will find his labors abundantly repaid in the interest the classes will take when they come to the use of books and the recitation of lessons therefrom. It will be easy to carry the young mind from the object lessons, thus supplied, to the contemplation of the remotest parts of the earth. Imagination will readily frame pictures of far-distant regions, guided by observations, induced by these preliminary instructions.

DAY AND NIGHT.

One of the most interesting lessons that the teacher can bring before his class in this oral method, before books are used, is the explanation of the phenomena of day and night. The observation of the youngest child has prompted the question, What makes day, and what makes night? The teacher may introduce this subject so pleasantly and simply that all will be interested in it, and all may comprehend the principles that govern the phenomena. Though no schoolhouse should be without charts or globes, it is assumed for the purpose of elementary instruction that, as is frequently the case, the teacher is without any apparatus, except only such as he can construct from materials at hand. He states to his class that the earth has two motions; one is a motion on its axis, and the other is a motion through space around the sun. Let him take a spheroid-shaped object, as an apple, or turnip, or potato, or an onion, or a ball such as the boys use to play with, and attach it to a string two or three feet in length. By holding the end of the string in such a position that the ball will be suspended and easily seen by all the members of the class, he may twist the string in his fingers and thus produce a revolution of the spheroid on its axis. This illustrates the meaning of the first definition. If he will move his hand so as to describe circles, he will cause the spheroid to move in the same way, and if, at the same time, he will twist the string, two motions will be produced; one is the revolution on the axis, and the other is the motion through space. Of course the teacher will think of explaining to the children, that the earth is not thus suspended by a string, but that it moves in space and is held in place by invisible forces.

The class is told that the revolution of the earth on its axis produces day and night. This may be illustrated as follows: Let the teacher provide himself with some large spheroid. If he is in a city or manufacturing town, he can procure at a turner's shop, for a few cents, a piece of wood turned in the required form; if he is in the country, he can obtain a large turnip or a pumpkin; or if unprovided with either of these, a ball, or a hat with a round crown, will answer the purpose. He explains to his class that east and west, north and south, points of the compass, are relative terms applying to the earth and its sphere. Place upon the middle of the spheroid, between the poles, the letter E, and call that point east; directly opposite to this attach the letter W, and call that point west; midway between the E and W attach some object, as a strip of paper, to represent a place inhabited by an observer. Let one of the boys in the class be stationed on the platform; holding the spheroid in such position that the letter E will be next to the boy, say to the class, Suppose that boy represents the sun; now, if men are residing here where this mark is—pointing to the object between the E and W—which way would they look to see the sun? The answer will be, Toward the east; and the question, What time of day is it when you look toward the east and see the sun? would bring out the answer, Morning. Now turn the spheroid so that the object representing the place of the observer is directly opposite the boy; the pupils will see that the observer then looks straight away from the earth, and will understand that it is noon to him; continue to turn the spheroid until the letter W is seen by the boy who represents the sun, and the pupils will perceive that the observer looks westward to see the sun, and will understand that it is then evening at that point. When the spheroid is turned so far that the observer is on the opposite side from the boy on the platform, it is impossible for him (the observer) to see the sun, and therefore the pupils will understand that it is night. As the spheroid is turned still farther, the observer will again be able to see the boy on the platform by looking eastward, and it is then morning.

By some such simple method every teacher may make plain to young children, what is very often not clearly understood by full-grown persons. If a teacher is provided with globes and orreries, maps and charts, and has skill to use them, such simple devices will be unnecessary.

THE SEASONS.

Another interesting lesson may be given on the seasons. By the use of the same spheroid provided for the previous demonstration, a teacher may give to his class a correct idea of how the seasons are produced by the revolution of the earth about the sun. Let him draw upon the surface of the spheroid lines, representing the equator and the lesser circles on the globe, explaining that the position of the earth is always such, that the axis inclines toward a fixed point in the heavens. Some object may be placed upon the teacher's desk to represent the sun, or a boy may stand upon the platform for this purpose; the teacher will explain that, when the rays of the sun strike the earth perpendicularly, they produce a greater heat, than when they strike it obliquely, just as a rod projected against a board perpendicularly strikes with greater force, than if it is projected obliquely. By holding the spheroid in such position that the axis will always incline in the same direction, and moving it about the object used to represent the sun, the teacher will illustrate how the rays of the sun in different parts of the earth's course, sometimes strike equatorial regions perpendicularly, and at other times portions north or south of the equator perpendicularly; that when the perpendicular rays are upon that portion of the earth south of the equator, and the oblique rays upon that portion of the earth north of the equator, the greatest heat is south and the greatest cold is north; that it is then summer south of the equator and winter north of the equator; that as the earth continues in its course and presents to the perpendicular rays more northernly portions of its surface spring approaches, and as the most northern latitudes pass under the perpendicular rays midsummer is reached, and then the earth, still passing on its course, presents more southernly portions of its surface to the perpendicular rays, and thus autumn and winter come upon northern latitudes. This can be clearly illustrated by simple contrivances within the reach of every school-teacher. They will add great interest to the study, and, in many instances, the uniqueness of the apparatus will do much to stamp durably upon the mind the truths illustrated thereby.

RACES OF MEN.

The ramifications of commerce into all parts of the globe and the construction of railroads in all parts of the country have induced such an intermingling of the races, that almost every school-district will furnish in its population two or more characteristic types of the human race. A set of photographs, lithographs or engravings representing the distinguishing features of races, may be purchased at small cost, and can be used as the subject for a very interesting lesson. The teacher, of course, should not attempt to discuss the finely-marked and questionable distinctions, but only those well-defined outlines in feature and character that can be comprehended by the class before him.

MAPS AND BOOKS.

After such a course of preliminary training, the class in Geography is prepared to take up the study formally from maps and books. The subjects treated of in the oral lessons may be rapidly reviewed from the text. The method of conducting recitations by questions and answers is the very worst that can be advised for teaching Geography to pupils of all grades, and should be abandoned. It is much better to require one pupil to describe the distribution of water on the earth's surface; another, the divisions of land; another, public improvements; another, the appliances of commerce. This brings the whole subject unitedly before the whole class, which is much better than to serve it up as hash. In what manner the study of any political or general or grand division of the earth's surface should be presented to a class has been fully described in another part of this work.

Geography presents many suggestive lessons, and a teacher should constantly be on the alert to take advantage of these suggestions and enlarge upon the lesson in the text. History contributes many interesting incidents to Geography. Geology and Astronomy likewise bring rich treasures to this department of learning. It is, therefore, especially one of those branches of common-school studies in which teachers preeminently are required to *teach*, and not merely to exercise classes in questions and answers.

MAP-DRAWING.

In the study of political divisions, where boundaries are to be defined, as also in the study of the grand divisions, where general features are to be impressed upon the mind, where cities are to be located and points made interesting by historic events are to be indicated, exercises in map-drawing afford the best discipline, and tend to fix definitely and durably in the mind those outlines and features in Geography which it is desirable to remember, and at the same time it excludes masses of insignificant trash which not unfrequently comprise the bulk of the text-books on Geography. Both positively and negatively, therefore, map-drawing is a valuable and desirable exercise. It may, moreover, be introduced to pupils who are at that age, when inability to grapple with the more intricate branches of common-school learning gives time for map-drawing, which is then made to serve as well for recreation as for instruction. What is usually termed Physical Geography will be considered in the chapter on Geology and other sciences.

CHAPTER X.

METHODS OF INSTRUCTION.—Continued.

BOTANY.

HE elementary facts of the science of the vegetable kingdom are everywhere visible. No study presented to pupils of the medium public-school age is more interesting or attractive than that which describes these facts, classifies and combines them in a science. How to observe intelligently the growth and decay of vegetation, how to distinguish one class of plants from another, the ability to name herbs, shrubs and trees at sight, can be acquired at a very early age, and will be among the most useful and agreeable knowledge that is gathered in the whole course of common-school study.

Two methods of studying botany are presented:

1st. That which begins with the seedling rising from the ground and observes its development into a full-grown plant.

2d. To begin with full-grown plants and study their differences and similarities so as to classify them in accordance with well-marked characteristics into classes, orders, tribes, genera and species. A strict adherence to the natural order in scientific investigation would require the pupil to pursue the first method—that is, to begin with the seedling just rising from the ground, and to trace the changes produced until the ripened seed, similar to that which was deposited in the ground, is reached. But for the purpose of common-school learning, and to bring the subject fully within the comprehension of the pupils, the second method should be adopted—that is, children who have observed the differences in vegetation, and are familiar with the outward form of many plants, should be instructed to systematize their observations, to inspect closely objects presented, with the view of ascertaining which are like and which are unlike, and in what respect they are like and unlike.

The study of botany is clearly divisible into two periods—the period of observation and the period of classification. In the first period pupils should collect facts, and in the second period they should classify the facts in accordance with similarities of form and structure. The facts of botany are plants and their parts. The classification of botany is in *series*, *class*, *order* or *family*, *tribe*, *genus*, *species*, *variety*.

This division of the subject gives rise to two series of lessons—one series in which pupils may learn to distinguish the forms and parts of plants; another series in which pupils may learn to compare plants and to classify them, beginning with the largest division and proceeding downward through the smaller divisions.

FIRST SERIES OF LESSONS.

The study of botany should begin in the spring or summer, when vegetation is abundant. The first lesson should be on some familiar plant, as a violet or a buttercup, found in all parts of the United States. Suppose, then, the teacher has provided for the lesson a few specimens of the buttercup, full plants, with all the parts well developed. Hold the plant in the left hand, so that all the members of the class can see it, and with the right hand point to the parts. To begin with, here is a root; note its shape; it is slender, branching, or it is bulbous; the class should be questioned as to what other plants have roots similar in form, and the teacher may name a few most familiar. Proceed next to examine the stem: it is single or it is branching; the branches grow out from the main stem opposite to each other, alternately, or in whorls; the stem is soft, fleshy, succulent, or it is hard and woody; it is hairy or smooth; it is solid or it is hollow. All these particulars must be determined. Here are leaves; what is their general outline? Have any other plants leaves like these in shape? The leaves, like stems, grow out opposite to each other, alternately, or in whorls; the edges of the leaves are regular or irregular; hold a leaf up to the window and see if veins or branches are visible; these veins are parallel or netted. Here are flowers, also; examine one of them and discover its structure. These glossy yellow parts are called petals—do not forget that name, *petals;* there are five of them, and when taken together they form the corolla. But, see, here is something under the corolla that has been overlooked; here are five green leaflets, or something that resembles leaflets; these are *sepals;* the five taken together form the calyx. The calyx is a seat or base for the corolla; the sepals are supports for the petals; the sepals are green, like the stem and leaves, the petals are richly colored, a golden yellow. The five petals are not arranged directly over the five sepals, but they grow out alternately with them. On the top of the flower, filling the cup formed by the corolla, are a great number of fine, delicate parts; upon close examination it is found that these are not all of the same form; there are two forms of vegetable organs here, and there are a great many of each kind; first, in the outside circles of this little cup is one kind and in the centre is another kind of organs; these on the outside are called stamens, those in the centre are called pistils. Count the stamens and pistils in the specimens.

The superficial examination of a plant as here indicated will suffice for one lesson. In another lesson other specimens of the same *tribe* or *genus* should be examined and the differences pointed out. Of the buttercup genus, there are species with smooth stems and species with hairy stems; there are bulbous roots and branching roots; there are also marked differences in the leaf forms, stems and flowers, which will afford materials for two or three lessons.

The knowledge acquired in the study of the structure of plants of one family prepares pupils to advance to the comparison of specimens from two or more distinct families.

The mint family is found in nearly every part of the United States early in summer, and is, therefore, a very proper subject for a lesson of comparison. The stems of mint are square, the leaves are opposite and the corolla is single and lip-shaped. The mustard family will supply convenient specimens to be introduced with the mint family. In these the stems are round, and have a pungent, watery juice; the flowers have four sepals arranged in the form of a cross, and four petals arranged in the same manner, and the leaves are alternate. The differences between the members of these two families, therefore, are very marked. The plants of the mustard family will also be known by their seed-pods, such as are found in the cresses, in pepper-root, in the mustards, in the shepherd's purse, in pepper-grass, and, what is still more common, in the radish. Radishes and mint are familiar to most children; these differences will, therefore, be studied with interest, and that there is no family resemblance or natural relation between these two orders of plants will be fully comprehended.

These lessons in the general comparison of plants may be extended so as to include specimens of the herbs, shrubs and trees most numerous in the vicinity and most marked in their characteristics.

SECOND SERIES OF LESSONS.

A second series of lessons may be so framed as to comprise a more close examination of specimens of the same order, tribe or genus. Let the neighborhood be thoroughly scoured by the pupils, who should be instructed to collect spe cimens of some well-marked family—as, for example, the mint family—ascertain how many varieties can be found in the vicinity of the schoolhouse, examine these closely, in order to point out their characteristic differences, and thus exhibit the features that determine the classification.

In these lessons of the second series, a teacher may with propriety introduce technical names of leaf forms. The veins of leaves may be examined more closely to discover differences in arrangement. The general outlines of the leaves should be distinguished—whether they are *linear*, that is, long and narrow; *lanceolate*, that is, lance-shaped; whether they are *oblong*, that is, two or three times as long as broad; whether they are *elliptical*, or oval, or wedge-shaped, or heart-shaped, or kidney-shaped, or arrow-shaped, or halberd-shaped, or shield-shaped. By examining a number of leaves it will be found, that the points in different leaves are unlike in form of termination. Some are acute, ending in an acute angle; others are *obtuse*, that is, have a blunt or rounded ending; others are retruse, or have a shallow notch in the end; others are obcordiate, that is, are inversely heart-shaped; others cuspidate, round, but tipped with a sharp point like a tooth. Leaves differ also in the outline of their edges. Some have smooth outlines; others are saw-toothed on the margin; others have deep, round dents or scallops; others are jagged in the margin, having sharp, deep, irregular teeth; some leaves are lobed, like those of post oak; others are deeply cleft, like some varieties of the maple. All these varieties are put in one class, and are called simple leaves. Others are put in the class of compound leaves; these are such as are composed of a number of parts, as the leaves of the locust or the pine family, and the variations in such general characteristics should be pointed out, the teacher being careful never to present so much in any one lesson as to cause confusion or to engender discouragement. Technical names describing forms of leaves will be enough to begin with. As classes advance and become more apt in marking distinctions, names can be given denoting these distinctions, and, by frequent references, the repetition of the name and its application to the feature indicated by it, will make both familiar.

The lessons in the first and second series might with profit be given to an entire school, and occasionally an afternoon might be spent in examining the vegetation in some field or grove near the schoolhouse. In such excursions, the school may be divided into classes, and a leader appointed for each class, whose duty it would be to see that none of the children stray away or miss the instruction given in the excursion. The older pupils should be directed to assist their younger companions in finding specimens of plants, and to instruct them how to distinguish the most marked features in different classes. In this way the whole school will be interested, and numerous specimens will be collected which can be carried to the school-room for close inspection and classification. By pursuing this method all members of the school will soon become familiar with the name of every herb, shrub and tree in the neighborhood; the pupils will, in turn, instruct their older brothers and sisters, and even their parents, and thus a general diffusion of useful knowledge will take place, for which the teacher will receive due praise.

CLASSIFICATION.

When the facts of the science of botany shall have been collected by a system of observations as above described, the time and the materials for classification are at hand. The technical names belonging to the parts and features of plants should be learned in the first and second series of lessons. As the facts are collected they should be named. This will enable the teacher to speak intelligently of characteristics which determine classification. Moreover, when a fact or a phenomenon is observed, it should be named, so that the name and the fact may be at once associated, and the one may be used to indicate the other. The pupils have already learned that plants reproduce themselves by seeds; that in most plants the seeds are matured in the flower, or in the seat of the flower; that other plants do not bear flowers, but produce, instead of seeds, spores, which grow on the leaves. Of these the ferns furnish a good example. The first classification of plants is based on this feature—plants that bear flowers and plants that do not bear flowers. This distinction divides the whole vegetable kingdom into two series, flowering plants and non-flowering plants.

By examining the structure of plants it will be found that the fibres of the stem in some grow in circles, like the oak, chestnut and other familiar trees—that is, an additional circle of woody fibre is added to the stem of the plant each year. Many annuals—such plants as grow up in the spring and decay in the fall and winter—have the same structure, the fibres are arranged in circles; in other plants fibres are arranged in bundles, as is the case in the palm family and in the lily family. By cutting the stem of a common lily, or of sorghum or broom-corn, it will be seen that the fibres of which it is composed are arranged in close bundles, and not in circles, as are the fibres of the buttercup, the rose and geranium. Plants in which the fibres of the stem are arranged in circles are called outward growers, because the stem increases by adding one layer of fibre to another. Plants in which the stem-fibres are arranged in bundles are called inward growers, because they increase by putting up through the middle of the stem additional bundles of fibre. This gives rise to another classification among flowering plants. The first class are the outward growers and the second class the inward growers. The teacher may give the technical names of these classes as *exogenous* and *endogenous.* In the first class the leaves are netted-veined, in the second class the leaves are mostly parallel-veined. This is sufficient for one lesson in classification. Now let the pupils be instructed to scour the fields and woods to gather specimens of exogenous and endogenous plants, binding those belonging to each class in bundles.

The second lesson may be given on the divisions of exogenous plants. The teacher may explain without giving the technical distinctions that Class 1 contains two sub-classes; the second of these sub-classes contains all plants with the exception of conifera or cone-bearing plants, of which the pine is an example. Sub-class 1 contains plants with flowers having a calyx and a corolla, as is seen in the example of the buttercup, with separate sepals and petals present. It also contains plants in which the petals are united into one, and plants whose flowers have neither calyx nor corolla, or only a calyx; this gives rise to three Divisions. Division 1, in which the calyx and corolla are present, with the parts distinct and separate; Division 2, in which the calyx and corolla are present, but the petals of the corolla are united in one piece; Division 3, in which the corolla is always, and the calyx sometimes, wanting.

To illustrate this lesson, the teacher should have present specimens of each of these subclasses and divisions. Before the class is dismissed, the pupils should be instructed to collect a number of specimens representing each subclass and each division, binding them in separate bundles.

A third lesson may be based upon some of the orders or families under the first division of exogenous plants. Those flowers with numerous stamens—that is, those in which the number of stamens is more than twice the number of sepals—may be taken up. Among these will be found some families that are already familiar—the rose, the buttercup and the portulacca. The members of these families will be distinguished by the differences in the arrangement of calyx and corolla, the number of petals, the position of the stamens and the position and form of the leaves.

The subject of classification is thus fairly introduced; the process is now essentially the same throughout the study.

A class thus instructed is prepared to take up the "Manual of Plants" and trace characteristic features through the entire classification, so as to acquire facility in observing and accuracy in distinguishing, that will enable them to ascertain the name of any plant that may be presented for their determination. Throughout the whole study the teacher must lead his class; whenever he discovers symptoms of confusion of ideas, or inability to classify as far as the instruction has gone, he should immediately begin a thorough review, should present new illustrations, and thus rediscuss the subject in such a manner as to clear away the difficulty and renew the zeal and confidence of his pupils. If the teaching is thorough, there is no danger of teaching too much; as long as there is a family of plants undetermined, as long as there are herbs, shrubs or trees in the neighborhood not named by the class, the search and classification should go forward.

Though the spring season is the proper time

in which to begin the study of botany, a teacher taking charge of a school, which opens in September, should take advantage of the closing weeks of the season of vegetation to instruct his pupils in this beautiful and attractive branch of natural history.

By giving directions for the drying and pressing of specimens of plants and arranging them in herbariums, properly labeled, with time and place of gathering the plants noted, he will ensure an ever-increasing interest in this study and thereby give additional value to his labors, by providing for contributions to science. Every State might thus obtain, through its department of public education, a complete collection of the vegetation found upon its soil.

GEOLOGY.

According to Prof. Hitchcock, a division of geology of practical value is as follows: 1st. Scenographical geology, or an account of rocks as they exhibit themselves to the eyes—in other words, an account of natural scenery.

2d. Economical geology, or an account of rocks with reference to their value or their application to the wants of society.

3d. Scientific geology, or the history of rocks in their relations to science or philosophy.

In the language of geology, the term rock em-

braces all the materials, including the solid compact forms of rocks, as well as soils, clays and gravels that cover the solid parts. This signification should be explained to the whole school at the very beginning of the study of geology. As a branch of learning adapted to the scope of public schools, the study of geology must be confined to the first and second divisions of the subject as above made.

Natural scenery is produced chiefly by the arrangement of the rocks that constitute the surface of the earth; it is true, the surface is usually covered with vegetation, but this as often detracts from as it adds to the general effect. The first lessons in geology, therefore, are lessons on scenery—are lessons on the materials composing the surface of the earth as they are presented to the eye. In the walls of the schoolhouse, in the road or street, in the fields adjoining the school-lot, will be found specimens of rocks differing widely in their appearance; some are white, some blue, some red, some gray; some are smooth and regular in fracture, others are rough and irregular; some are soft and some are hard. Here are facts observed; these should be named and classified. If the school is in the rural districts, children, in walking half a mile to and from school, will observe in the road-bed, or in the fields on the side of the road, that the ground in some places is of a yellowish color, in other places of a reddish color, in some places stiff and clayey, in other places loose and sandy; or they may pass over ledges of rock in place. At one point this rock may be white, smooth, satiny in its fractures; in another it may be white, smooth and glassy in its fractures. If pieces of rock from such ledges be taken and rubbed together, it will be found that one is scratched and cut on the surface, whilst the other remains unchanged; that one is calcspar, which is lime, and the other quartz, which is flint. The neighborhood may be examined to ascertain at how many points limestone may be found in place, and at how many points quartz may be found in place. If there are mountains in the vicinity, in all probability one side of the mountain will show limestone and the other side sandstone or granite. Ores, coal, marble, felspar, and generally stratified rock and unstratified rock may be found in close proximity in many neighborhoods throughout the country.

These are surface phenomena that are observed; they should be studied and classified; this will afford agreeable, easy and profitable work for a school at every session. If the school is in a city, the specimens of building stone that can be found in almost every school-district will afford illustrations of facts in geology. The accessible suburbs and the great parks, fruitful in botanical and geological illustrations, should be visited and studied systematically and regularly. The banks of streams, especially where they have cut through hills and mountains, or where they impinge against hill and mountain slopes, will frequently afford views of rock in place, so that pupils can see how one stratum is laid upon another in the structure of the earth. The deep cuts made in the construction of railroads lay bare many hidden secrets, which pupils from schools in the country and in city should be invited to examine and study. Every schoolhouse should contain a case of shelves and drawers, into which specimens of all the rocks, both solid and disintegrated, in the district, should be arranged, properly labeled with the name of the specimen and place where it was found. A system of exchanges may be introduced throughout the county, so that each schoolhouse would soon contain a complete cabinet of geological specimens representing all the formations in the county; these exchanges might be extended through the State, so that all the formations in the State would be represented in the cabinet of each school-district, and the school-department at the State capital, by a requisition upon the several districts, might procure for the State a complete geological and mineralogical cabinet, in which would be represented the soils, rocks and minerals of the State. Under such a course of instruction the pupils in every school-district would be made thoroughly familiar with the names of the rocks and minerals in their respective neighborhoods.

An examination of the mountains, hills, valleys or plains in the vicinity of the schoolhouse will give profitable recreation, and the acquaintance with their geological structure that will thus be acquired will constitute part of the most practical and useful knowledge that pupils will carry from the school-room into the active concerns of life.

The whole subject of Scenographical geology may be successfully taught without the use of text-books.

Economical geology.—When the names of the rocks and their positions in the surface formations have become familiar to the pupils, a knowledge of their uses will be easily and speedily acquired.

In the studies of the uses of rocks it will be convenient to divide them into two classes: first, those that are in solid masses, and, second, those that have become disintegrated into soils, clays. etc. The teacher is supposed to be familiar with Scientific geology, including the chemistry of geology, for he will have occasion to draw frequently upon his resources to explain the relative qualities of soils and their adaptability to purposes of agriculture, so as to explain, generally, the classes of vegetation that grow most luxuriantly on each variety of soil found in the neighborhood, and also the uses of clays and sands in the manufacture of brick, earthen or delf ware and glass. Rocks in masses are chiefly useful as building material, differing very greatly in value for such purposes. The rock in place in every neighborhood may be examined and its relative value as a building material determined and noted in the records of the school-district. This work may also be accomplished more thoroughly for the class without the use of a text-book than with it. The effects of water, air, sunshine and heat upon soils and rock, whether in solid masses or in disintegrated forms, should be explained by the teacher, and examples of these operations of the elements should be pointed out in the geological excursions made in the neighborhood.

Geology, like botany, is a study for the summer season. It may be taken up at the opening of a school in the fall and pursued as long as practicable, when it may be laid aside and its place supplied by the study of Physiology or

Natural Philosophy. Scientific geology is, with few exceptions, beyond the scope of a public-school course. Where there are graded schools or high schools, the whole subject of geology can, after a period of observation and classification as above described, be taken up and thoroughly studied from text-books.

CHAPTER XI.

METHODS OF INSTRUCTION.—Continued.

GRAMMAR.

EARLY writers on the subject of English Grammar adopted the theory, that it is the business of grammarians to construct a language. They followed the same order of construction that is observed in the study of the natural sciences. They presented elementary facts and treated of their names, forces and uses; they set forth principles and rules that are to determine the combinations and uses of these elementary facts. They multiplied definitions, rules and exceptions, and then required the student of the English language to carry these definitions, principles, rules and exceptions into the analysis of the literature of the language, chiefly to ascertain, whether the authors of that literature constructed their composition in accordance with the rules laid down by grammarians, or if not this, then to apply these rules to the composition of authors in order to show that the theory of the language agrees with the structure, or, conversely, that the structure of the language agrees with the theory. The erroneous assumption of the first writers on English grammar has been copied and strictly followed by their successors, and, therefore, there are no text-books on English grammar of any practical value as school-books. With erroneously-constructed text-books and the blind dependence of most teachers upon these books, grammar, as taught in the public schools, and, in fact, in all schools, has been one of the most disagreeable, incomprehensible, discouraging studies with which pupils, students and teachers have been embarrassed and annoyed.

In a strict sense, grammar is the science of language. It is the business of the grammarian, not to construct a language, but to explain a language that is already constructed and in use. The pupils who enter the public schools, and have arrived at that age and degree of advancement, at which the study of grammar may with propriety be taken up, have attained a certain degree of skill and facility in the use of the English language.

Those who are members of families, in which language is used correctly, come to the schoolroom with habits of correct speaking. Those whose associations have been with parents and friends, who speak the English language incorrectly, come to school with habits of incorrect speaking. The language of the first class—namely, those who have been reared to use speech correctly—will not be improved by the study of grammar. The errors of the second will not be corrected by the study of grammar, but the force of habit will be counteracted by imitation, and by judicious criticisms from the teacher in recitations and discourses.

In presenting the subject of English grammar, or the science of the English language, as a study in the public schools, the question to be determined is to what extent this science may be profitably studied by those pupils, who constitute the masses in these schools, and who are not likely to attend any other institution of learning.

If, in the spelling-classes, the uses of capital letters and punctuation marks have been noted—as should be the case in spelling from dictation and discourse—and if in the reading-classes the structure of sentences, the meaning of words and the uses of punctuation have been properly studied, there is little remaining to be taught on the subject of grammar, to pupils in the public schools, that properly comes within the scope of these institutions.

It is exceedingly doubtful whether the subject of grammar can be taken up as a study in these schools, without consuming time that might be much more profitably devoted to other branches of learning. Nevertheless, in order to assist those who deem it essential that the "mother language" shall be studied in the schools of the people, a practical method of instruction is here set forth.

THE FIRST LESSON IN GRAMMAR.

First, then, it is the duty of the writer and teacher of English grammar to explain the structure of the language, with the use of which the pupil is to a very considerable extent familiar. Pupils have already learned, in the reading-lessons, what is meant by the term sentence—a collection of words expressing a complete thought. "Merchants sell goods," is a collection of words declaring a fact, conveying an idea, expressing a thought. Here are three words composing this sentence. Let the teacher, in his first lesson to a class entering upon the study of grammar, write this or a similar sentence on the blackboard. There are two principal parts to every sentence. Before a fact can be declared, or an idea expressed, there must be a subject concerning which the fact is to be declared or of which the idea is to be expressed. That is, before a man writes or talks he must have something to write or talk about; this something of which he is to write or speak is called the subject. In the sentence before us, of what do we speak? Clearly of merchants; the declaration is concerning merchants, and therefore merchants is the subject.

The second part of every sentence is evidently that which is said of the subject. If a man wishes to write or to speak, it is not only necessary that he shall have a subject to write and speak of, but it is also necessary that he shall write or say something about that subject. That which he says of the subject is called the predicate. In this sentence before us it is said of "merchants" that they "sell goods;" therefore sell goods is the predicate. The sentence is thus divided into two principal parts, of "merchants," the subject, and "sell goods," the predicate. Now let the teacher write upon the blackboard, as rapidly as possible, six or more sentences, and require the pupils to name the subject and the predicate in each. Let him then invite the pupils to suggest sentences of their own, which he may also write on the blackboard, so that the subject and predicate may be distinguished.

This is a process of analysis. The language is taken up, and the learner proceeds, by analysis, to resolve sentences into their parts, for the purpose of discovering the relation of those parts; beginning first with the largest divisions the process is to arrive, by a series of subdivisions, to the simple elements. The teacher may indicate a general form of analysis, which may be followed by the pupils in separating sentences into subject and predicate; thus, "Merchants sell goods" is a sentence, because it is a collection of words expressing a complete thought. "Merchants" is the subject, because it is that of which an affirmation is made. "Sell goods" is the predicate, because it is that which is affirmed of the subject. The teacher should require each member of the class to bring to the next recitation twelve simple sentences written on paper, with a perpendicular line drawn between the subject and the predicate of each sentence. This much will be sufficient for one lesson.

SECOND LESSON.

In the second lesson the teacher may explain that, when two or more sentences expressing a complete thought are united, they are, when taken together, called a compound sentence. There are, therefore, two classes of sentences, simple sentences and compound sentences. The drill in the second lesson should be the analysis of compound sentences by separating them, first into simple sentences and then stating the subject and predicate of each. Let the teacher, before dismissing the class, require of each member to produce at the next lesson twelve original compound sentences with a perpendicular line drawn between the subject and the predicate. If the teacher will impress upon the mind of the pupil that, in writing a sentence, it is only necessary to select a subject and say something about it, the class will easily perform these written exercises.

THIRD LESSON.

In the third lesson the work of analysis may be extended one step farther—that is, the subject and the predicate may be resolved into parts and these parts may be considered each by itself. Take the original sentence, "Merchants sell goods;" the subject is comprised in a single word, "merchants," and that word is a name applied to a class of persons engaged in the business which is indicated by the word. The predicate is composed of two words, "sell" and "goods." The first word, "sell," explains what the "merchants" do—namely, that they sell or dispose of, for a consideration, something. "Goods" is the general name employed to describe what the "merchants" "sell."

Take another sentence: "Good girls study diligently;" here the subject is composed of two words, "good" and "girls;" the predicate is also composed of two words, "study" and "diligently." The first word, "good," describes the kind of girls of which the affirmation is made; "girls" is a name applied to a class or to a collection of individuals; "study" tells what these individuals do, and "diligently" tells how they do it. Let the teacher, if he has not before him a convenient number of examples in some text-book, provide a number of sentences, which the class should analyze by defining in a general way the office performed by each word in the sentence, always requiring the pupil to begin by dividing a sentence into subject and predicate, to proceed by first considering the words in the subject, and after that the words in the predicate, stating the office performed by each. Require each member of the class to write six sentences in which both subject and predicate shall comprise two or more words. These original sentences may be brought to the next recitation, and be made subjects of analysis.

FOURTH LESSON.

The pupils have now learned that in the subject of every sentence there is a word which stands as the name of a person or thing. The time has arrived when the fact may be communicated to the class, that these words representing persons or things are called *nouns;* let the class point out the nouns in the sentences they have written, and in numerous other sentences, which the teacher may either cite from the text-book on grammar, or write upon the blackboard, or point to in the charts employed in the spelling- and reading-lessons. Not only point out the words that are nouns, but give a reason why they are nouns; thus, "merchants" is a noun, because it is the name of a class of individuals. City is a noun, because it is the name of a large town. Potato is a noun, because it is the name of a vegetable. Acorn is a noun, because it is the name of a nut. Rose is a noun, because it is the name of a flower. Bone is a noun, because it is the name of a kind of animal matter. Permit the pupils to give their own reasons, the teacher taking care simply that the reason is sufficient to determine the fact that the word is a noun. Require the members of the class to write twelve sentences with the nouns underscored.

FIFTH LESSON.

In the predicate of every sentence there is also a leading word, which describes the leading word in the subject by telling what it does, by indicating its action, state, condition or being; this word the teacher may inform his class is called a *verb*. By referring again to the original sentence, "Merchants sell goods," the word which describes "merchants" by stating what they do is "sell." It, therefore, is a verb—is a verb, because it describes the subject of the sentence by indicating action. The sentences written by the class should be re-examined and the verbs therein pointed out. They should not simply be pointed out as verbs, but a reason given by each pupil for calling the words selected verbs. The requirement to write twelve sentences should be repeated, with the additional direction that the verbs should be underscored.

SIXTH LESSON.

In the sixth lesson adjectives should be defined, pointed out and reasons given. Thus, "Good girls study diligently." "Good" is an adjective, because it modifies "girls" by indicating their character. After the sentences in the possession of the pupils have been examined and the adjectives therein pointed out, teachers should require the production by each pupil of twelve or more original sentences, each containing an adjective underscored.

The adverb, the pronoun, the preposition, the conjunction and the interjection should be made subjects of lessons, in which they should be treated in the same manner that has been pursued in the study of nouns and other parts of speech. The sentences in each exercise should be analyzed, and all the facts, as far as learned by the pupils, stated in each analysis, beginning with the division of the sentence into subject and predicate and ending with the naming of the part of speech to which the word belongs, and stating a reason for the classification. The writing of sentences in illustration of every lesson is the most valuable part of the exercises given, and must, therefore, be insisted upon throughout the study of grammar.

LESSONS ON THE VERB.

In the preceding lessons the pupils are supposed to have learned to distinguish words found in sentences, to classify them into "parts of speech," and to use those parts of speech in the construction of original sentences. A class that has been thoroughly drilled in these exercises is prepared to proceed to the study of sentences, for the purpose of determining more minutely the relations of their parts and of the words composing them to each other. It has already been discovered that in every sentence there must be a subject, the principal word in which is a noun; every sentence also has a predicate, the principal word in which is a verb describing the principal word in the subject. The leading noun in the subject of the sentence is called the subject of the verb which describes it. A sentence may be composed of two words, one in the subject and one in the predicate; or, both subject and predicate may comprise a number of words, and hence there are incomplex and complex subjects and predicates.

In analyzing a sentence, therefore, it is first separated into subject and predicate, and then each word entering into the composition of the subject is considered separately in order to see in what manner it modifies the principal word in that subject, and likewise every word in the predicate is considered separately so as to see in what manner it modifies the principal word in the predicate.

Sentences are usually classified as declarative, imperative, interrogative, exclamatory and hypothetical. These should be clearly defined, so that pupils will be able to distinguish at sight to which of these classes a given sentence belongs. In every sentence action or existence is expressed. Wherever action is expressed there is necessarily an agent producing the action, sometimes also a recipient which receives the effect or action produced by the agent.

The principal verb used in a sentence expressing action, that is received by a recipient, is classed as a transitive verb, and those verbs in sentences in which the action is limited to the agent, but does not extend to a recipient, are called intransitive verbs; thus, in the sentence, "James struck Charles," the verb struck represents the agent "James" as producing an action which took effect upon "Charles"; *struck* is therefore called a transitive verb; it is a transitive verb, because the action produced by *James* is carried across, is transferred, to *Charles*, where it takes effect. In the sentence, "Boys play," the verb *play* represents an action which is wholly limited to the agent *boys*, producing that action, but does not represent action as taking effect upon a recipient; it is therefore called an intransitive verb, because the action is not carried across, transferred, to a recipient. After this distinction has been thus drawn, a class should be required to write a number of sentences containing transitive verbs, and a number containing intransitive verbs, and at the next recitation they should be required to state whether the verbs used are transitive or intransitive.

It frequently occurs that the agent producing action expressed by the verb does not precede the verb, as in the example given above, "James struck Charles," but follows the verb, as is the case when the sentence is reversed, "Charles was struck by James." These two forms of the verb are called, by some grammarians, "voices." The direct form, that is, that which is preceded by the agent and followed by the recipient, is called the "active voice" of the transitive verb, and that in which the verb is preceded by the recipient, and is followed by the agent, which is connected to it by the preposition *by*, is called the "passive voice" of the transitive verb. In the sentence, "Our hopes flatter us," *flatter*, being preceded by the agent *hopes* and followed by the recipient *us*, is called a "transitive verb of the active voice." In the sentence, "We are flattered by our hopes," *are flattered*, being preceded by the recipient *we* and followed by the agent *hopes*, is called a "transitive verb of the passive voice." The teacher should write on the board, or provide from books, twelve or more sentences containing transitive verbs. He should require the pupils to change these from one form of the transitive verb to the other, and to give the reason why one form is the active voice and why the other form is the passive voice in each sentence. At the close of such an exercise, the direction to write sentences should be renewed. They must be sentences containing transitive verbs written in both forms. The intransitive verb should be made the subject of a separate lesson, which should consist in writing a number of sentences employing that form of the verb, and in analyzing these sentences in the manner already indicated.

LESSONS ON NOUNS.

It will be profitable to suspend the lessons on the verb at this point for the purpose of considering nouns, so that the knowledge of the pupil can be applied in the analysis of sentences. The lessons must be carried on without variation of the principles which govern their selection and treatment. The division of nouns may be taken up in one recitation, and the distinctions of proper, common, abstract and collective nouns clearly marked and then illustrated in original sentences. Person, number, gender and case should each be made the subject of a lesson, each lesson to be illustrated by the production of original sentences. Following these distinctions of nouns, the person and number of the verb may be taken up and defined.

Parsing, by which is meant the mentioning in order of the peculiar variations of a word and the relation it sustains to other words, may now be introduced to the class. It should be a daily exercise, pursued, of course, only as far as the knowledge of the pupil is prepared to carry it; thus, at this stage of the progress of the study of grammar, the pupils may parse every noun in the sentence by stating its kind, person, number, gender and case. Verbs may be parsed by stating whether they are transitive or intransitive, whether of the active or passive voice, what nouns they agree with in person and number. The analysis of sentences should be continued throughout the study of grammar.

Mode and Tense.—One of the most difficult subjects for a class in the study of English grammar is the distinction of modes and tenses of verbs. Much confusion and embarrassment will be avoided by taking up one thing at a time, and making it thoroughly familiar to the class by analysis, by parsing and by writing original sentences. Refuse absolutely to proceed one step beyond what is familiar ground to the whole class. It is of small consequence how deep and how dense the darkness is in front, if all is clear in the rear. But whenever there is a step taken into that darkness, the light disappears, and darkness is all around; then every effort to proceed simply makes matters worse.

In studying relative pronouns, the variations and distinctions of adjectives, the force of conjunctions, the relations of phrases, infinitives and participials, it is of the utmost importance that the principle so often insisted upon here, of attempting but one thing at a time, shall be observed. Classes of pupils who have arrived at that age, when but one or two years more can be given to common-school studies, may thus, with a degree of profit, be led through a limited course in English grammar. It is much better to proceed only so far as to the distinction of the parts of speech and their relative uses in the construction of sentences with a clear comprehension, than to attempt the study of the numerous variations of words and their intricate combinations and complexities in the construction of sentences, with no prospect of having a clear idea of anything, though a text-book shall have been gone through with.

From what has been said on the subject of teaching grammar, it will be seen that the method here recommended supersedes the established practice in nearly all schools, public or private, of all grades. The basis of the study as here set forth is the sentence, and one feature or characteristic is taken up at a time and disposed of, and the lesson given one day is illustrated at the next recitation in a number of original sentences prepared by the pupils.

It is not necessary to study grammar in order to acquire the ability to speak and write correctly. The great masses, who receive only so much education as can be given in the public schools, do not learn to speak and write their "mother tongue" by the study of grammar. This branch of learning, therefore, in point of utility, takes rank far below arithmetic, which in turn ranks below the material sciences. If some author, comprehending the work necessary to be done, and possessing that courage which would permit him to depart from received methods, would treat the subject of English grammar logically and concisely in a text-book for the public schools, there would then be less objection to introducing it there as a study; until that shall be done, its introduction is more likely to result in confusion of ideas and distaste for study than in any good to the girls and boys in the public schools. Skillful teachers may do much to compensate for the short-comings of book-makers; nevertheless, the introduction of a branch of learning in the schools of the people that, up to this time, has utterly baffled its advocates and authors in their countless efforts to arrange it properly in lessons for juvenile learners is, to say the least, an act of very questionable propriety.

CHAPTER XII.

METHODS OF INSTRUCTION.—Continued.

ANATOMY, PHYSIOLOGY AND HYGIENE.

HUMAN anatomy, which is the part of the general science of anatomy that may appropriately, nay, that should, be introduced into public schools as a study, treats of the structure of the human body. Physiology is a term applied to the science which treats of the uses of the different organs that enter into the anatomy of the body. Hygiene relates to the laws by which the healthful action of these parts is governed and preserved.

The human body consists of systems of organs. There is a system of bones, a system of muscles, a system of digestive organs, a system of circulatory organs, a system of respiratory organs and a system of nerves. There are secretory organs, lymphatic vessels, vocal organs, organs of taste, of smell, of sight and of hearing. These several systems entering into the composition of the human body are to such an extent distinct from each other, that they may be taken up and studied without reference to any particular order. It is immaterial whether the bones, the muscles, the digestive organs or the circulatory or respiratory organs are studied first, but it is material that each system, as it is taken up, shall be thoroughly studied and clearly understood before another is presented.

In order to obtain a knowledge of the framework of the human body, it may be well to begin the study of anatomy at the system of bones. A teacher may procure specimens of bones of animals; he may obtain these fresh from the butcher-shop, so as to show how they are bound together at the joints by ligaments. Describing the joint in the class, he can discourse upon its structure without any especial reference as to whether the muscular system, the tendons and ligaments have already been studied. He can explain at the time sufficient for the purpose of the demonstrations, and show how bones are bound together, and how muscles are attached to them. He may explain the composition of bone, the effect heat and cold, age and exposure, have on it.

Numerous text-books on anatomy admirably treat of bones, their formation, combination and place in the human frame, and describe the bones of each part separately and clearly. For a class supplied with these books, the teacher need only be careful to provide suitable illustrations that will enforce the lesson upon the comprehension of the pupils, and enable them to carry the ideas of the school-room from the books out into fields of practical observation. This method must be continued, not only in the lesson on bones, but also, through the lessons on muscles, circulatory, respiratory and other organs.

Muscles, as developed on the leg of a rabbit, a squirrel, a frog or a chicken, will admirably illustrate the manner in which the fibres are bound together in bundles and how they are extended into tendons and attached to the ligaments at the joints.

A set of anatomical charts should be at hand, from which the teacher can demonstrate the relations of different parts in the bony structure, the functions or uses of bones, and give to his class a much more correct idea of the relative position of the parts of the human system than he would otherwise be able to do. How bones are affected by habits of sitting, walking and dressing should be explained at the end of a series of lessons on this subject.

The Muscles.—The lessons on the muscles of the human body, their structure and arrangement should be conducted very much in the same manner as are those on the bones. No part of this science can be profitably studied by a class on the question-and-answer method. Pupils should be required to describe parts of systems, as the bones or muscles of the head, the bones or muscles of the leg, the feet, the arm, or of the hand. One pupil may describe the bones of a certain part, another the muscles, and a third may state the functions or uses of the bones and muscles. As the class advances, the veins and arteries, the nerves, the skin, and the hygienic principles that govern the development and health of the parts and organs under consideration may also be described by the members of the class.

This whole subject has been so practically presented by the authors of text-books, that there is little occasion for doing more here than to urge, most earnestly upon the school authorities and teachers, its introduction as one of the branches of learning to be studied in every school.

The study of arithmetic may be cut short, grammar may be altogether excluded, exercises in reading may be less frequent, but the study of anatomy, physiology and hygiene, the study of our own bodies, the organs of which they are composed, the nature and uses of these organs, how to secure their development, how to preserve them in health, how to treat them in case of accident or disease, is of so much and of such vital importance to all men in every condition of life, that it should be a work of supererogation to plead for its introduction as a special study in the schools of the people.

NATURAL PHILOSOPHY.

Natural Philosophy, so far as it treats of the application and extent of forces met with in the operations of life, should be made the subject of study in public schools. The power of water, the power of steam, the power of air, of electricity, and the power of mechanical contrivances everywhere encountered, should be made familiar to the young, so that they may be understood, whether they are to be used, resisted or controlled. The possession of apparatus to illustrate principles in Natural Philosophy is absolutely necessary, if any considerable amount of good is to be accomplished by these lessons. Where such apparatus is not supplied by the school authorities, teachers, by the exercise of an ordinary amount of skill and ingenuity, may contrive pieces of apparatus that will be useful in illustrating many lessons. A cord and two or three pulleys, two or three small spheres, rings, spheroids and small cog-wheels can be obtained at a hardware store or at some machine-shop, and will serve to demonstrate many of the most interesting and useful propositions.

If there are manufacturing establishments in the vicinity of the schoolhouse, the teacher should take his pupils thither and explain the mechanical forces employed in the operations carried on there. If water supplies the power, lessons on hydrostatics may be illustrated; if steam, then the steam-engine, its parts and its mode of working, the extent of its power and the contrivances for applying its forces to turning machinery, should be explained. The differences between stationary and locomotive engines, between high-pressure and low-pressure engines, can be practically studied in the presence of these machines. The use of the blackboard to sketch the parts of engines and machines should be resorted to frequently, so that before pupils are taken to observe the actual working of a steam-engine they will be conversant with the internal arrangement of the parts and the application of steam to them. The power of water-currents and air-currents may be frequently observed at all seasons of the year and at all places. It is only required that the teacher will seize upon the occasions, and turn the phenomena to practical use as illus trations of the principles set forth in the text-books.

In the study of Natural Philosophy the constant aim should be to carry the principles obtained in the books out into actual operations. The use of the lever is so common that pupils will be delighted to understand the relative strength and force of the mechanical power, that may be gained by the use of a lever in different positions.

This branch of the physical sciences has been so successfully treated in text-books that teachers will find little difficulty in arranging lessons systematically for the instruction of classes, and if these lessons are thoroughly taught—not recited by systems of questions and answers, but fully explained and illustrated by such apparatus as the teacher may be able to procure—and if the principles that are learned are afterward recognized in actual use—that is, if pupils are trained to determine in their minds the philosophy of action as observed in manufacturing operations, in agricultural operations, in all the motions and rests where mechanical forces are applied,—this will be made one of the most interesting branches of learning taught in the public schools.

CHEMISTRY.

The science which treats of the nature of the elements, the laws of their combinations, their affinities and uses, is so closely allied to everything that is within us and around us, that its elementary principles should be made the subjects of study in the public schools. It is admitted that chemistry, in its largest sense, cannot be successfully studied without the use of apparatus and appliances far beyond what can be supplied to teachers in the public schools; nevertheless, the names of the solid and fluid elements, their general nature and uses which enter into the composition of the human body and of the earth, into all solid and liquid matter, may be taught to pupils who receive their education in the public schools. The names of the metals, their characteristics and their uses, the names and properties of the elements of the most familiar compounds, as water, air and salt, will be studied with pleasure and profit. The relations of acids and alkalies, the effects of heat on all matter, the effects of sunlight, of air, of water, in their numerous combinations and relations, may be made subjects of observation and explanation that will be within the comprehension of such pupils as are found in the public-school classes.

If apparatus can be procured to illustrate the effects of electricity, to generate gases by simple methods, and to perform some of the most simple and striking experiments with the natural elements, the use of such apparatus will contribute greatly to the interest and value of the instruction. If it is found impracticable to introduce the study of chemistry into mixed schools, a teacher may provide himself with suitable text-books on this subject, from which he can prepare short discourses or lectures on the most important lesson in the science. Such lectures can be delivered to the whole school at appointed intervals, and should be followed by questions on the facts and principles set forth therein. By this method, during each school-term, many of the important principles may be taught to a school. The pupils may thus be led into habits of observation and research, that will enable them to read understandingly and to discourse intelligently on the operations of nature. It is admitted that such instruction is likely to be superficial, yet it is the only instruction on these subjects the large majority of boys and girls in the United States can possibly receive in their school-days. Those whose education will not extend beyond the public-school curriculum will be greatly benefited thereby, though it be superficial, and those who are so fortunate as to receive the advantages of a higher education will not be affected injuriously by this preliminary and general view of the elements of sciences which, in their subsequent progress, they will be required to study more minutely and thoroughly.

CHAPTER XIII.

METHODS OF INSTRUCTION.—Continued.

PENMANSHIP.

THE suggestion made in the chapter on teaching the alphabet, that every child in school should be provided with a slate and pencil, is here repeated. Children accustomed to the use of a pencil in forming the letters of the alphabet, and in sketching pictures on their slates, attain a considerable degree of skill in the art of drawing before regular lessons in penmanship are taken up. Though letters, as used in writing, differ very widely in form, there are really but few simple elementary forms employed in the art of penmanship. The practice of every child should begin by exercises on these simple elements, taking the simplest of them first. The method formerly pursued was to set copies for children in straight lines, and after a certain degree of facility was acquired in forming these lines, copies of hooks were set, and these were followed by ovals. When such copies are given without any explanations, they are arbitrary, and children fail to see the benefit to be derived from marking over many sheets of paper in straight lines, hooks and O's, but if the teacher will explain and illustrate on the blackboard that the straight line and the hook and the oval are really parts of letters, and that one or more of these parts are used in the formation of every letter in the alphabet, the lesson will be invested with a degree of interest that cannot otherwise be given.

Though the slate and pencil are admirably adapted to the execution of elementary lessons in drawing, they should not be employed in lessons in penmanship. The object of these lessons is to exercise the pupils in forming letters on paper with pen and ink. Children should not be permitted to attempt to combine the elements of letters into letters before they are able to form the elements with a reasonable degree of accuracy and regularity.

Few schools are now without a series of copy-books projected upon one of the numerous systems of penmanship that have been constructed for the education of children in this art. The old custom of setting copies by the teacher is superseded. The copy-books now in use are arranged on a progressive system, beginning with the simplest elements and rising by a gradual system of combinations up to a regular practice in forming words and sentences. The teacher is, therefore, required simply to criticise intelligently the efforts of individual pupils, pointing out errors in such way as will indicate the difference between faulty and correct penmanship.

Lesson on the Blackboard.—Before the writing-lessons for any term are begun, and frequently during the term, the following principles should be explained by the use of the blackboard: All the small letters found in writing are compounded of three elementary principles—the *i*, the *o* and the *loop*. The *i* principle is employed in forming *i, u, w, r, t, n, m, v, x* and *s*. The *o* principle is employed in forming *o, c* and *e;* by a combination of the *i* and *o* principles *a* and *d* are formed. The *loop* principle is used in combination with the *i* or the *o*, and enters into the forms of *l, b, h, k, j, y, z, g, q, f* and *p*.

This explanation of the forms of letters indicates a proper arrangement of progressive lessons.

The first series of lessons should be on the *i* principle in its variations and combinations with itself.

The second series of lessons should be on the *o* principle and its modifications.

The third series of lessons should be on the combinations of the *i* and *o* principles with each other.

The fourth series of lessons should be on the *loop* principle above the line, below the line, and a combination of these positions.

The fifth series of lessons should be on the combination of the *loop* with the *i*.

The sixth series of lessons should be on the combination of the *loop* with the *o*.

The exercises in these lessons will be in letter-forming; the letters are next to be combined in words. The first series of copies should consist of words requiring the use of only the *i* and *o* principles. After pupils have acquired reasonable skill in writing such words, copies of words requiring the *loop* principle may be given.

Capital letters should be taken up after pupils are able to write words distinctly in small letters. Capital letters are also constructed of three elements: the chirographic curve, or line of beauty; the stem, or *T* principle, and the *O*. The curve enters into the forms of *A, N, W, P, B, R, S, L, I, J.* The *T* enters into the forms of *T, F, Z, H* and *K.* The *O* enters into the forms of *O, C, E, G, D, Q, V, W, X* and *Y.* This classification suggests three series of lessons in the elements and their uses. These lessons must be so arranged as to introduce one new element or combination of elements at a time. Finally will come lessons arranged progressively, in which capitals are used with small letters in framing words and sentences.

It is especially important that the teacher would enforce habits of neatness in penmanship, in the care and preservation of copy-books.

Three things are to be attained in lessons in penmanship:—First, the ability to write legibly; secondly, to write rapidly; thirdly, to write neatly. Legibility is an essential requisite, for what cannot be read had better not be written. Letters should be formed regularly, not crowded together nor too widely separated, but uniformly spaced.

For practical purposes rapidity is a very desirable acquisition. For all business purposes this accomplishment stands much higher than that of beauty in style of execution. The ability to write in that regularity of form which gives great beauty to executions in penmanship is useful for technical, special and professional purposes. In business affairs, however, a general neatness in the appearance of the written page is what is required. This will be attained only by forming letters regular in size and uniform in style, keeping the page clean, writing every word legibly, spacing all words regularly and preserving a harmony in the shading of letters, so that one part of the page shall not appear black with ink and another part faint and indistinct. Whilst this sort of neatness must be insisted upon, the teacher must avoid the extreme of sacrificing rapidity of writing to the demand for skill in extreme beauty of execution. Rapidity is of more use to the mass of writers than the ability to write beautifully.

Freedom in the use of the pen is attained by frequent practice in forming large letters requiring the movement of the whole arm. Exercises of this kind are provided in the copy-books of all the systems of penmanship now in use. Wherever the teacher discovers a want of freedom of motion in the execution of any pupil, he may correct this by requiring such pupil to return to the practice of these general arm-and-finger movements.

DRAWING.

In point of time drawing precedes penmanship. By the use of the slate and pencil small children are taught to draw from copies on charts or on the blackboard, to form at first the simplest letters of the alphabet, and to rise gradually to the execution of the most complex. They learn to sketch pictures of animals, plants, articles of furniture, diagrams, trees, flowers, maps and the parts of machinery. These lessons may be continued after the children have passed from this simple use of the slate and pencil to the study of mathematics and the sciences. In the study of geography, the recommendation has already been made, that map-drawing should be regularly practiced. In the study of mathematics, diagrams are frequently drawn.

Teachers should be prepared to instruct all pupils in public schools in elementary rules and principles of drawing. A knowledge of these principles, and skill in the art of using them, will prove to be valuable attainments in many positions in life. Mechanics constantly employ this art in their business; carpenters, engineers, architects and machinists are draughtsmen, or must employ draughtsmen; physicians, miners, farmers, and even lawyers and clergymen, will very often find it useful to be able to convey by sketches and drawings, what it might be very difficult to make plain by verbal explanations.

All drawings consist of straight lines. It is, therefore, necessary to acquire, first, skill in drawing such lines.

The first series of lessons should be on straight lines. First, simply a straight line; then a combination of two straight lines in various forms, as meeting at right angles, meeting at acute angles, meeting so as to form one angle, meeting so as to form two angles, crossing each other so as to form four right angles, crossing so as to form acute and obtuse angles. Another lesson may be given on combinations of three straight lines, another on combinations of four straight lines in various forms. These lessons may be extended as the age and skill of the pupils shall require more complex exercises.

A second series of lessons should be given on curve lines, as semi-circles or smaller arcs of circles, on forming complete circles, forming ovals, also combinations of curve lines, drawing curve lines parallel to each other and crossing each other in every conceivable form.

A third series of lessons may be given in combinations of straight and curve lines. After this, pictures of real objects should be given to be copied, with instructions how to proceed. The objects at first should be simple, as doors, gates, boxes, ladders, benches, chairs, houses, and the like; gradually more complicated lessons may be given, such as drawing pictures of animals, plants and machines, and finally lessons on drawing pictures of the objects themselves.

Lessons on drawing, arranged progressively, have been published for the use of schools, and these are usually accompanied by a series of models. The picture is found in the book, which the pupil may copy, and after such exercises shall have continued for a sufficient length of time, the pictures are removed and the objects themselves presented. Pupils are required to make pictures of these objects. This is a valuable exercise, and is what is required in actual business. In the application of the art of drawing, the object is represented either in reality or in the perceptions, and a picture of it is to be produced on paper or tablet. Where such regularly-prepared lessons are not provided, the teacher may improvise lessons and present a number of suitable objects, of which pictures can be made by the pupils on slate or paper.

This is one of the branches of learning that may become so fascinating to teacher and pupil as to encroach upon the time that would be more profitably expended in the acquisition of other and more useful knowledge. Only the elementary principles should be taught in the public schools, and sufficient practice given to attain a reasonable facility in sketching simple objects. This will be sufficient for ordinary unprofessional uses. Persons, who enter vocations wherein this art is to be very generally employed, will find it necessary to study it beyond the limits of what is practicable in the public schools.

MUSIC.

Vocal music has become one of the essential public-school branches. Music in all schools is necessary for purposes of recreation, for purposes of discipline, for purposes of culture. It is more useful as an exercise than as a study, but in order to enable pupils to engage in the delightful exercise of singing, some system of instruction whereby they will acquire the ability to read music at sight must be adopted.

It is not more difficult to teach pupils to understand musical notation than it is to teach them to understand arithmetical notation. The terms employed in music are similar to those employed in reading. Every musical sound has pitch, length and force. The pitch of a musical sound is indicated by its position on the musical staff; the lower sounds are placed on the lower part of the staff, and the higher sounds on the upper part of the staff. Let a teacher draw five parallel lines on the blackboard, thus ☰.

These lines and spaces represent pitch in ordinary musical composition. A character called a note is employed to represent each sound; the position of the note on the staff indicates its pitch. Let the teacher write notes on different parts of the staff, beginning below and rising from the lower line to the upper line. Then let him sound with his voice the pitch of the tone indicated by one of these notes; then the pitch indicated by another, and thus ascend and descend the scale slowly, giving the same time and force to each note, varying it only in pitch. Pupils will readily understand the difference between high notes and low notes, and easily execute the distinction in vocal efforts.

The teacher may explain that the lines and intervening spaces in the diagram on the board are designated by certain letters of the alphabet, numbering from A to G. These letters should be written upon the diagram on the blackboard in their proper positions as found in musical composition.

If the teacher will call the attention of the pupils to the fact that the letters occupying the spaces in this diagram spell the word *face*, he will enable them to fix the position of the letters on the staff correctly and durably on their minds. The four fingers and the thumb of the hand may be cited as an illustration of the musical staff; beginning with the little finger and the one next to it, placing "F" in that space, "A" in the second space, "C" in the third space, and "E" in the fourth space. The letters on the lines are the letters of the alphabet which, when written in their natural order, come between those which are found in the spaces. Thus, in the alphabet after *f* comes *g*, after *a* is *b*, after *c* is *d* and after *e* is *f*, which is found on the upper line as well as in the lower space of the staff. What is of more importance, however, to the pupil, and of more practical use in school, is a knowledge of the musical scale, running from the keynote below through the scale of the octave to the keynote above. It will be found advantageous to designate the tones in the scale by numerals, beginning at the keynote and calling it 1, and writing the figures in regular order, 2, 3, 4, 5, 6, 7, and indicating the keynote at the top of the scale by the figure 8. Write on the natural scale on the blackboard an octave of notes, from C on the ledger line below to C in the third space; write on the left-hand side of these notes the numerals from 1 to 8; on the right hand side of the notes, write the names usually given to them in the scale; thus:

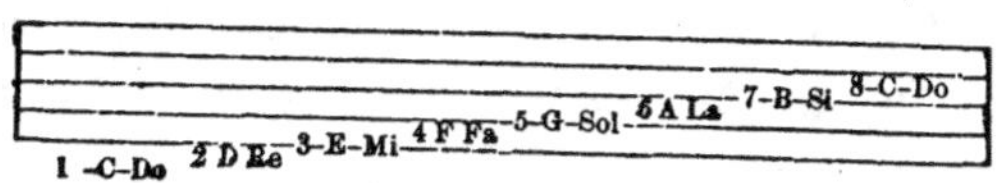

From this diagram the pupils may learn that, whilst absolute pitch is indicated by position on the musical staff, relative pitch—that is, how much higher or how much lower one note is than another of a known pitch—may be represented by numerals and by syllables. By thoroughly enforcing this idea of representing relative pitch by numerals, the teacher will make it possible for his school to read music rapidly that is written upon the blackboard in numerals.

Length of Sounds.—The length of sounds is indicated by the *form* of note. By reference to any piece of musical composition, it will be seen that the notes on the staff vary in form; by singing the piece the teacher may illustrate the meaning of these differences of form. Pupils must be taught to distinguish between whole notes, half notes, quarter notes, eighth notes and sixteenth notes; this can be accomplished best by the use of the blackboard. The principles of measure and time, employed in writing and executing compositions in music, can also be fully demonstrated by the use of blackboard diagrams and the voice.

The transposition of the scale by the use of sharps and flats can be explained so as to be comprehended by pupils at the age of ten years.

For school-room uses it is not necessary to understand the transposition of scales. Explain the meaning of the term "keynote;" it is 1, or "do," in the major scale. If, therefore, pupils are able to find the keynote of the scale of a piece of music, they can without difficulty read the notes in the piece, giving to each tone its proper pitch and length. The teacher may, therefore, state without explantion that, when one sharp is found on the staff at the beginning of a piece of music, the keynote is on *g;* when two sharps are placed there, the keynote is on *d;* when three sharps are used, the keynote is on *a*, and when four sharps are used, the keynote is on *e*. One sharp, *g;* two sharps, *d;* three sharps, *a;* four sharps, *e:* "God Deluged All Earth." Here are four words the first letters of which indicate the keynotes in sharps. The use of flats gives keynotes as follows: one flat, *f;* two flats, *b;* three flats, *e;* four flats, *a:* "Father Baker Eats Apples." These four words in their initial letters indicate the keynotes in flats.

An extract, or complete piece of music, should be written on the blackboard. Suppose it is part or the whole of the familiar church tune, "Old Hundred."

The teacher proceeds to explain: First, that the cleff indicates the position of the letters on the staff; secondly, that the presence of one sharp indicates the keynote is on *g;* third, that the figures indicate double measure, two half notes in each measure. After these facts have been explained, question the class as follows: In what key is this piece of music written? What is the name of the first note? The name of the second note? Of the third? The fourth? Fifth? Sixth? Seventh? Eighth? The answers may be given in concert, individually, or both. In what kind of notes is this piece written? Are the tones represented all of the same length? Why? The class should repeat the notes by name until all the members can do it rapidly. The teacher may then sound the keynote, *do*, and require the class to sound it with him. Sound it several times; then sing, in slow, regular time, all the notes on the staff, thus: Do-do-si-la-sol-do-re-mi. The correct pitch of each note must be given in the tone of every pupil. This lesson should be practiced by the whole school until every pupil can sing it correctly by naming the syllables. It should then be sung in the syllable la, thus: la-la-la-la-la-la-la-la. Words of a hymn may now be applied to these tones. The whole school may sing in full, harmonious voice, "Be thou, O God, exalted high." The teacher may now complete the tune and exercise the school in singing it.

The pitch of the several tones in this tune have thus far been represented by position on the staff; they may be represented by numerals. The keynote is 1 of the scale, and other numerals up to 8 are used to indicate the position of notes in the scale. The tune may, therefore, be written as follows: 1 | 1 7 | 6 5 | 1 2 | 3. In the tune "Old Hundred" the notes are all of the same length, but if notes of different lengths are found in a tune, a teacher can, by dots and points over the numerals, indicate the length of sounds. Every tune is written on the basis of some note, as whole, half, quarter. Some one length of note is, therefore, of more frequent occurrence; using that note as a standard of length, only those that are longer or shorter need be marked. The vertical lines drawn at intervals between the numerals also aid in determining at sight the time to be given to notes between them. The active powers of perception and imitation will enable pupils to catch a tune, as it were, intuitively. If a tune is written in numerals, and the teacher sings a short division of it, requiring pupils to repeat it several times, then another and another, until all the parts of the tune have been sung, the whole school will take up the piece and sing it through by note, by the syllable la, and afterward in appropriate verse. Words of tunes may be repeated by the teacher so slowly that the pupils can write them on paper, to be preserved for use.

Every school should be provided with music-books containing suitable tunes; frequently, however, this will not be the case, and when books are present other tunes may be added to the supply by the free use of the numeral system of notation. As pupils advance the general principles of rhythm, melody and dynamics may be explained and illustrated in singing. What is chiefly wanted, however, is exercise in singing, the instruction necessary to enable pupils to read music may be given in such simple and easy lessons as not to mar the pleasure of singing, and to an extent that will suffice for all practical uses in school, at home and in church.

In giving music lessons a teacher must be vivacious, cheerful and of good heart. The soul of music must find lodgment in his soul; his countenance must say to the school so unmistakably as to require no interpreter, "It is good to sing." "As in water face answereth to face, so the heart of man to man." The little hearts and the larger hearts will join in the cheerful exercise of singing if pleasantly invited and cheerfully led.

CHAPTER XIV.

METHODS OF INSTRUCTION.—Continued.

HISTORY.

HISTORY may be studied by first taking a comprehensive and general view of the historic field, and proceeding thence to the study of special or local history, or beginning with local history, by studying fragments, and rising through the history of governments, nations and periods to general history. Either method may be adopted. For advanced pupils and for adult readers the first named is the natural course. Children may be interested in fragments of history, in biographies of distinguished men, in stories and incidents of localities, at an age when general history would not be relished and could not be comprehended.

By whatever method history is studied, it is important that, at some period in the study of fragments, the epochs, the periods, the history of nations, governments and people, by some system of general and comprehensive classification, be so arranged and bound together as to enable pupils to remember the relative order of historic events, such as the founding, the progress and the fall of nations and governments, without the necessity of recollecting arbitrary dates.

Facts in history are not governed by recognized laws that bring them under a classification that determines their place in the progress of events. They are not susceptible of the close and systematic classification that is attainable in the material sciences; they may, nevertheless, be so connected in great cycles as to aid the student in determining, instantly, at what particular epoch or period the history of any particular nation or people or events belongs. Whether, therefore, the pupils have prosecuted the study of history by the first or second method above indicated, a general survey must be made for the purpose of classifying and combining historic events in the order of their occurrence.

If it is proposed to study history by the first method, then the general survey should be introduced at the beginning. If history has been or is to be studied by the second method, the general view should not be presented until a sufficient number of fragments are possessed by the student to make classification desirable.

The beginnings of few nations are known to history. Until nations have assumed some form peculiar to themselves, and have asserted some individuality distinguishing them from neighboring nations, they do not enter the horizon of history. Before they have reached that period centuries may have passed, of the events of which no records are preserved.

The prehistoric period is the age of fable; obscurity and darkness reign over the mutations of men and their transactions. The science of language has recently passed the boundary of this unexplored region, and has penetrated the hitherto impenetrable darkness of the ages of unrecorded changes. It has discovered many ancient landmarks, erected by migrating nations and peoples and languages, and from these monuments of the unknown past, philology has suspended ever-burning lamps to guide students of history to the fountains of historic events, the cradle of races of men, the beginnings of civilization, whence issued the streams that flowed out to all parts of the earth.

The developments of the science of language has resulted in the discovery that there was a great prehistoric cycle of civilization, whose centre and beginnings were in Upper Asia. A people and language, the parent of all nations and of all tongues in times immemorial, dwelt in this region and became the ancestors of Indians, Persians, Celts, Germans, Slavons, Italians and

Greeks. Out from this centre of population flowed successive waves of migration. Guided by the lamps of philology, which thus light up numerous stations on the highways of nations, we are able to pass far beyond the true historic period and arrive at what seems to have been the cradle of all nations. Tracing the lines of migrations backward, it is found that these all point to the table-lands of Armenia in Asia, as the place of genesis, whence issued the families of all nations.

The first great body that emigrated from Armenia into Europe was the Celts, who passed over the northern parts of Europe; this wave was followed by the Teutonic or German emigration. The Germans pushed the Celts forward to the extreme western bounds of the continent. Following the Teutonic came the Slavonic wave of migration, which in turn pushed the Germans westward and southward, and made the whole of Northern Europe the home of the Slavons. The Celts were pushed out into the islands on the western coast of Europe, and the Germans settled in the central and western parts of the continent. These three peoples together are the immediate ancestors of the nations and languages of Northern Europe.

The second succession of waves of migration

spread over Southern Europe. First came the Pelasgi, and secondly the Greeks. The first of these, the ancestors of all the Italian races, were pushed forward to the Pillars of Hercules, and spread over the southern part of Europe, on the shores of the Mediterranean Sea. The second wave settled in South-eastern Europe and its people were the fathers of the Greeks. The migrations into other parts of Asia and Africa from Armenia are not so distinctly marked. The population seems to have spread out in great circles, widening its territory, rather than projecting distinct currents.

The languages of the East are of one family, of which the Hebrew may be taken as a type. The languages of the West were more diversified. The Celtic became the foundation of the English, the Teutonic of the German, the Slavonic of the language of the Russians. In the South, Latin and its offshoots and the Greek were the typical languages.

In receiving its population, therefore, Asia and Northern Europe were in advance of Southern Europe, but in the development of civilization and the cultivation of the arts and sciences, Eastern and Southern Europe were in advance of their older neighbors.

The history of a nation begins at that epoch in its existence in which civilization develops an individuality, that asserts itself as a unity. History, therefore, treats of the progress of civilization from country to country, and from people to people, rather than of the dissemination of population over the earth. Civilization first came into historic recognition on the southern shores of the Mediterranean Sea; it passed around the east end of the Mediterranean and along the northern shore until it reached the Atlantic. This completed the first great historic cycle—the cycle of the Mediterranean civilization.

This historic unity is sometimes called "Ancient History," or the "History of the Ancient World." It is the history of civilization among the Mediterranean nations—the history of the Egyptians dwelling on the southern shore, the history of the Syrians on the east coast and stretching inland to the Euphrates, and the history of the twin nations, the Greeks and the Italians. The successive centres of the civilization of this cycle were at Thebes, Carthage, Athens and Rome. The nations represented by these culminating points, and embraced in the Mediterranean cycle, were the first to attain a noble civilization, and to elaborate and develop the distinguishing qualities of human nature, which have since their first evolvement characterized all civilized peoples.

After the lapse of centuries new peoples in

the North loomed into the horizon of history, overran the nations of the south and transferred the centre of civilization from the Mediterranean to the Atlantic Ocean. A new epoch in the mutations of nations is reached; out of the perished and the perishing civilization of the Mediterranean nations buds a new era. A new cycle of culture is formed, and the Atlantic nations become its theatre of influence. This new cycle is usually entitled "Modern History." In it, civilization was developed in the Atlantic nations, or those nations settled north of the Mediterranean zone, and who found their outlets on the Atlantic; passing northward on the eastern shore of the ocean, it reached all the peoples on the mainland and on the islands off the coast. At the close of the fifteenth century of the Christian era, civilization was carried across the Atlantic, and, after the lapse of fully one hundred years, made lodgment on the western coast of that ocean.

All the civilized nations of Europe vied with each other in efforts to settle and civilize America. Two centuries of earnest and intelligent labor have been given to this work. From the seacoast civilization spread inward until the whole continent was explored, and states, provinces and governments were established where, at the beginning of the sixteenth century, savage tribes of men roamed through an unbroken wilderness. This overspreading of Western and Northern Europe and of America, bringing the nations dwelling there under the influence of civilization, constitutes the Atlantic cycle in history. The Pacific cycle has already begun. Historic civilization has established itself on the American shore of the Pacific ocean, and is making rapid inroads upon the ancient exclusiveness of the nations residing in Eastern Asia. When the arts and sciences, known to civilized nations, shall have found a welcome in the islands of the Pacific, in the nations of Southern and Eastern Africa, in India, China and Japan, the Pacific cycle will be complete.

All historic epochs and periods are embraced in these three great cycles, the Mediterranean, the Atlantic and the Pacific. It is only necessary, therefore, for students of history to carry in their minds the date at which civilization began on the Mediterranean, the date at which it was transferred to the Atlantic and the date at which it reached the Pacific, and the course it took in its progress on the shores of these great waters, in order to determine, generally, at what time any nation, or the people embraced within the geographical limits thus described, became a civilized and an historic people.

Three comprehensive charts, constructed on

this principle, may be so arranged as to indicate the path of civilization in its course among nations, in passing through these cycles, and note the dates of marked periods and epochs. Such charts could be used as the bases of a series of lessons in history, so as to determine at once a classification that would be an invaluable aid to the student, placing before him connectedly a synopsis of the history of the several nations that belong to each cycle. With this clear comprehension of a general survey of the historic field, pupils will have little difficulty in determining, both chronologically and geographically, the places of nations and peoples within the sphere of civilization.

With such an outline of history before them, pupils may read or study the history of nations in any part of the world; they may study fragments of history, as biographies of public men, histories of wars, histories of dynasties, histories of states, with a reasonable certainty that they will associate them with the histories of other nations, dynasties, wars, men and events of the historic cycle to which they belong.

The study of history when recited by questions and answers is a very dull and unprofitable exercise. It is far better to use some popular history of a nation, or a state, or a people as a reader for advanced classes. A teacher, by comments and questions in a reading-lesson in history, may fix in the minds of his pupils all important events, and associate them with other events that will give them a proper place in general history.

History, however, should be classed as a regular branch of learning to be studied in every school, studied in fragments, studied in epochs, studied in cycles. Pupils should be required to state the important events connected with periods, epochs and cycles. If fragments of history are to be taken up, they are always susceptible of methodical division and subdivision. In the recitation of these fragments, pupils should be required to state, in their own language, the leading events, their connection with other events and their effect upon the people in the midst of whom they transpired, as far as consistent with the scope of the lesson and the capacity of the learner.

The objection to the use of historic charts in schools is, that they contain so much that is minute and immaterial, and that cannot properly be taught from charts, that they are more likely to produce confusion than to lead to systematic classification. If charts projected on some such general plan as has been here suggested are not published, teachers may construct on a blackboard, or on large sheets of paper, or on skeleton maps, cyclical charts that will embrace the nations, governments and dates of important events belonging to each cycle. One such chart should comprise the Mediterranean nations, another, the Atlantic, and a third, the Pacific. To these charts every fragment of history may be referred, its time and place indicated, so as to give the pupil a more perfect classification and system of combination of historic facts, than it is possible to obtain by any other system.

These points, then, are important: First: Every school should receive from its teacher a general statement of the events embraced in each of the three historic cycles.

Secondly: History should be studied in all schools, and the recitations therein should be conducted in such manner as to cultivate habits of relating briefly and correctly the facts entering into the events, periods and epochs under consideration, and to associate them with other epochs, periods and events of the same historic cycle.

Third: If, by reason of any circumstance, history cannot be taken up as a regular study in any school, it should be introduced as reading-lessons for the advanced pupils, and into these reading-lessons, the teacher should infuse as much teaching of history as time, and capacity of the pupils will permit.

This method presupposes teachers to be reasonably well read in historic literature. It will be impossible to make the study of history in a school interesting, if the whole stock possessed by the teacher is only so much as he is able to extract from the foot-note questions in school text-books. There is no branch of public-school learning so susceptible of varied and interesting illustration, by the introduction of collateral and explanatory incidents, as the subject of history. A teacher should ever be on the alert to arouse the interest of his pupils by frequently surprising them with agreeable illustrations, not found in the text-book lessons. It will thus be of small consequence what particular history a class is studying in school. The intelligent, active teacher, making it merely a text-book of suggestions, will draw to it from all sides the history of the whole world, so that when a pupil shall have gone over, for example, the history of the United States, he will in reality have been taught the history of the world, with that of the United States prominently in the foreground. If the class is studying the history of a state—for example, the state in which the school is located—the teacher should make each recitation an occasion, not only to consider the events which transpired within the limits of that state, but also to exhibit what relations those events sustained to contemporary events in other parts of the United States, so that when a class shall have completed the study of the history of one state, its members will have a general view of the history of the United States, with that of the particular state in the foreground.

CHAPTER XV.

FURNITURE AND APPARATUS.

THE manufacture and arrangement of school furniture have been reduced to perfect system. Desks for the accommodation of pupils are so modeled as to be convenient and ornamental. The styles of good furniture are sufficiently numerous to accommodate every demand of service and taste. The school authorities, whose duty it is to furnish schoolhouses, should examine the several patterns of desks and select that which is best adapted to the wants of their school; either of the numerous approved patterns of combined desk and seat will give satisfaction. It is now so easy to obtain serviceable and elegant furniture, that school-officers should not be excused for lumbering up their rooms with clumsy, uncomfortable and inconvenient desks.

In the arrangement of seats it is a very general practice to place those for the small children in the front part of the room and increase the sizes of the desks toward the rear. A more perfect system is to place the low desks for small children in the centre section of the room, from front to rear, and the higher desks for the larger pupils, in two sections, on the sides of the room.

The following table serves to exhibit the relative length, width and height of desks convenient for all grades of pupils in primary, secondary and grammar schools. Rooms for mixed schools should be furnished with the required number of seats of the several sizes to accommodate all grades of pupils.

SIZES OF SCHOOL DESKS.

	Length of Desk and Seat.		Width of Desk Top. (Single and Double Desks the same.)	Width of Seat. (Single and Double Desks the same.)	Width from Desk to Desk. (Single and Double Desks the same.)	Height of Seat. (Single and Double Desks the same.)
	Single Desk.	Double Desk.				
Second Primary,	18 in.	36 in.	11 inches.	9 inches.	23 inches.	11 inches.
Primary,	18 "	38 "	12 "	10 "	24 "	12 "
Secondary,	21 "	40 "	14 "	11 "	28 "	14 "
Grammar,	24 "	42 "	16 "	12 "	32 "	16 "

APPARATUS.

Apparatus has become an indispensable part of school furniture. The principles, elements and facts of almost every branch of the common school curriculum, may be taught more successfully by the skillful use of numerous ingenious contrivances constructed for that purpose. The uses of charts, cards and blackboards to teach the alphabet, spelling and reading have been indicated in the chapter on Elocution.

In teaching the elements of arithmetic the arithmetical frame, blocks, charts and blackboards are useful; in geography, maps, globes and the mechanical combinations of spheres are valuable aids to both teacher and pupil. Penmanship has been reduced to such precise systems that charts and models are used to advantage in teaching the elements and composition of letters.

An expert teacher will find frequent occasion to improve on all the inventions of bookmakers and manufacturers of apparatus, and the school authorities, who fail to supply him with ample facilities in the way of convenient appliances, simply defraud the children of the advantages of the highest professional skill. Dull, book-bound teachers do not require apparatus—spirited, zealous, ingenious teachers do; and their spirit, zeal and genius appear to best advantage when supplemented by all proper conveniences for the full and free exercise of their power in forcing the knowledge they possess home to the minds of the pupils.

Apparatus Useful in Teaching the Alphabet.—By reference to the directions given on teaching the Alphabet from charts, and teaching with letter blocks, it will be seen that the system requires a full supply of simple apparatus for the use of the beginners in the primary schools.

A "reading case" has been constructed so as to contain a series of ten or more charts in such manner as will admit of the production of combinations of three words in great variety and in rapid succession, by the moving of slats. This apparatus may be used to advantage in exercises of pronouncing and spelling at sight, and also in the first lessons in grammar.

Apparatus Useful in Teaching Arithmetic.— The "numeral frame" is one of the oldest and commonest of the mechanical devices employed in teaching arithmetic. It consists of a frame inclosing twelve wire cords, each cord bearing twelve large wooden beads; the cords are of sufficient length to admit of the separation of the beads into distinct groups. This frame is convenient to exercise the beginners in arithmetic in counting objects, and in adding, subtracting, multiplying and dividing objects. Its use is so obvious and the exercises so numerous and simple that explicit directions are unnecessary.

The liberal use of the slate, blackboards and charts has elsewhere been urged. Every school should be provided with several small portable blackboards and a suitable frame upon which to place them before the school. Such boards will be employed by teachers in drilling classes and the whole school in standard exercises, not only in arithmetic, but also in music, geography, history, grammar, botany and other sciences. A full supply of charts will diminish the use of portable boards; nevertheless, an abundant supply of blackboard surface, of good quality and convenient form, is one of the essential requisites to every active, earnest teacher, and no school house should be deficient in this respect.

Arithmetical Charts.—Recently a great improvement has been made in arithmetical charts. By a mechanical device the old series of charts has been superseded, or rather the numerous single charts have been combined into one, which is so arranged on rollers, inclosed in a case, as to make it possible to present to a class, in rapid succession, simple combinations of numbers in almost endless variations. The use of such a contrivance enables a teacher, by simply turning a crank, to produce exercises in numeration, addition, subtraction, multiplication and division instantly, whenever required. This is, therefore, one of the greatest time-saving inventions yet produced by apparatus-makers, and should speedily take the place of the numerous series of single arithmetical charts now in use.

Solids.—Every school should be well provided with form models—samples of cubes, spheres, spheroids, cylinders, cones, prisms, pyramids, etc.—convenient for illustration. The uses of these forms are so obvious that it is surprising any school should be without them. They may be purchased at small cost, or made in the village "cabinet-shop."

Apparatus Useful in Teaching Geography.—The first lessons in geography consist in a study of the earth's surface. It is, however, but a very small portion of it that can be studied by direct observation; hence the necessity of employing apparatus to represent to the mind those portions that do not come under immediate observation.

The transition between the thing itself and the representation should at first be as slight as possible. It is less in passing from the study of the earth, by oral lessons, to the study on a globe than to a map; hence the study of the globes should precede the study of maps. The globe gives the true shape of the earth, which maps do not. It also represents the correct form of the bodies of land and water, which on maps are necessarily more or less distorted.

No school, therefore, should be without a globe. Next to the blackboard, this is probably the most important piece of apparatus used in teaching. From the globe, and without the use of maps and text-books, pupils may be taught the shape, the size and the surface composition of the earth, the names, relative location and the comparative sizes of the bodies of land and water lying on the earth's surface.

Map-drawing.—The most effective method of studying maps is by map-drawing; all necessary materials and apparatus for map-drawing should therefore be provided. A complete set of outline maps, properly mounted on rollers and frames, convenient for exhibition, suitable paper, books and pencils, are among the essentials in an outfit for a class in geography.

Tellurian.—A skillful teacher may succeed in teaching mathematical geography from a globe, but where rigid economy does not deny it, the school should be provided with one of those ingenious mechanical combinations of spheres known as the "Tellurian," "Lunatellus" or "Heliotellus."

These instruments are chiefly useful in teaching the revolutions of the earth around the sun and on its axis, the effects of these motions, the changes of seasons and their causes, the phenomena of day and night, the variations in the length of days and nights, the rising and setting of the sun and other terrestrial and celestial phenomena.

The apparatus important in the successful teaching of geography, therefore, is a globe, a complete set of maps and an instrument to illustrate the motions of the earth and celestial spheres.

Outline Maps.—The value of outline maps to the teacher and learner in geography is so well established that no school should be without them. As the object of these maps is to determine and impress the outline features of the general divisions, natural and political, those are best which adhere most strictly to this purpose. Detail in delineation is out of place. The maps should be so arranged in the school-room as to be convenient for use. The whole school may engage in exercises on the boundaries, capitals and prominent physical features in lessons that will interest and instruct all classes of pupils. By reference to the chapter on management,* teachers will find suggestions for the use of maps in oral instructions, reviews of past lessons and preparations for those to come.

A convenient device has been constructed whereby maps and charts are so arranged on frames, in a wooden case, that any map may be exhibited before the class at any time, while those not in use are protected from dust and exposure.

* Page 87.

Few schoolrooms have sufficient blank wall on which to suspend the maps that are needed by the teacher, and where there is room enough, it is usually above the blackboard. The charts suspended there are out of convenient reach, and consequently are seldom used. These difficulties are avoided by the use of this "map and chart case."

GENERAL OBSERVATIONS.

In addition to the articles already enumerated, every schoolroom should be furnished with suitable cases and drawers for the reception of books, apparatus, mineral and botanical specimens, with a clock, call-bell, class-bell and a few chairs for visitors. These are deemed necessaries; many other articles and appliances are highly useful, and, generally, school authorities who are so fortunate as to have secured the services of a successful, earnest, progressive teacher will do well to supply him with anything, that in his judgment would aid him in his efforts to instruct those who are sent to his school. Too often teachers are crippled, embarrassed and discouraged by the exercise of a mistaken economy on the part of patrons. The addition of the small sum of one hundred dollars to the cost of erecting and furnishing a schoolhouse would, in many cases, greatly increase the educating powers of the teacher, and thus add incalculable value to the expenditures already made. The mechanic, who compels his journeyman to work with dull and unsuitable tools, robs himself; the farmer, who permits his hired man to use heavy, inconvenient implements, and to drive slow and poorly-fed horses, defrauds himself; so likewise men, who withhold from a school-teacher the most approved appliances of his profession, simply, to that extent, diminish his power to serve them. It is the highest wisdom and the surest economy to supply proper implements and to exact the best services, not only in the art of mechanism and common labor, but also in the Art of Teaching

26

CHAPTER XVI.

HIGHER EDUCATION.

SYSTEMS of education as they now exist in all civilized nations have been propagated downward. Universities in Europe and colleges in America are the parents of all schools of lower grades, even the public schools in all parts of the country. The parent schools gave form, character and scope to all others. Means of education, objects of education, systems of education, courses of study and methods of teaching now in use, have been dictated, or suggested by universities and colleges, or they have been drawn from these and spread down over all that is below the fountain-head, carried forward by the ceaseless current of learning and schoolmasters that came from higher institutions.

It is inimical to the pure atmosphere of university and college culture to admit of the practicability of constructing courses of study with respect to direct utility. In the higher institutions the theory is, and correctly too, that study is prosecuted chiefly for purposes of discipline, that ideas of liberal culture are incompatible with limitations and technicalities imposed by special, or professional requirements. According to the university system, all persons destined for positions in the learned professions must first pass a course of educational training, calculated to discipline the faculties of the mind without the risk of limiting them to the narrow channel of a particular profession. Men whose preparatory education has been conducted with sole reference to use in the profession in which they are destined to engage, are, with rare exceptions, at the age of maturity, so wholly absorbed in the work of their chosen profession, that other concerns of life receive from them little or no attention. Such men are usually narrow, one-sided, impractical, in short, useless men for any purposes of society beyond their professional routine. It cannot be otherwise than painful to witness the blundering efforts and ludicrous conceits of men distinguished in some one of the learned professions, but wholly ignorant of many of the life problems requiring practical solutions in the progress of society and for the advancement of humanity.

The efforts of the ruling classes in educational

affairs in all nations have ever been put forth to provide, for young men, first, a liberal training by instructions in branches of learning chosen solely with reference to their influences as disciplining powers to all the faculties of the mind. The whole field of mental culture has been claimed on the one side by, and surrendered on the other side to, the authorities governing these institutions of learning. Technical schools, such as institutions of theology, medicine, law and polytechnics, have been encouraged as training schools, wherein educated men may be instructed in the sciences and arts of professions. It thus happens that the authorities, the faculties in universities and in colleges, regard all schools, not technical, as simply preparatory schools to their institutions. Academies are under the supervision of graduates from the universities and colleges; their system of teaching is that which was learned in these universities and colleges; the organization of private schools and of select schools is projected from the same initial sources; "high schools," graded schools, mixed schools, all schools, inherit their organizations, their courses of study, their methods of teaching, from the same general ancestry.

The assumption that public schools of all grades and academies are to be organized and conducted as preparatory schools for colleges and universities, has proven the source of incalculable mischief. Scarcely one in ten thousand of the boys and girls, who are in the public schools, ever apply to the colleges and universities for matriculation. The one who pursues the course of study, entered upon in the public schools, through the academy and into the college is benefitted thereby, but his ten thousand companions, whose education goes no further than the common-school course, would have derived much more benefit from their years of study, if the course of instruction had been constructed with reference to their wants; if the elements of the material sciences, as far as the limits of the course would admit of, had been made the subjects of study, the time would have been much more profitably expended. The colleges require for matriculation, the study of mathematics to a prescribed extent, the study of English grammar, the study of geography and the reading of a limited quantity of Latin and Greek. This requirement imposes upon the public schools of the lower grades the duty of instructing pupils in mathematics, grammar and geography, and upon the academies and high schools the duty of instructing the pupils in Latin and Greek grammar. It stands directly across the path of useful learning, and obstinately hinders the progress of a much needed reconstruction in the public-school course. When the true relations between the public schools and the higher institutions of learning shall have been determined, the province and scope of each defined, the people, the masses, who are educated in the public schools, will be able to procure such a course of instruction in their own schools, as is most consistent with the objects for which they were established—namely, to instruct the youths of the state in the elements of knowledge. The comparatively few, who are able to study science and literature for purposes of culture, will find ample opportunity in academies and city "high schools" to make that special preparation which is required for admission to colleges. But it is certainly imposing great injury upon the masses to insist, that their schools shall be restricted to the narrow duty of preparing boys for college, when only one of these boys out of several thousands ever enters the higher institutions. The public schools, established for the education of the millions, are unlike all other classes and grades of schools; the distinguishing feature of the public schools is breadth; the characteristic of other institutions is height and depth; the former seek to give useful knowledge to all, the latter seek, by a system of disciplinary studies, "to quicken the intellect and form it to habits of method, of analysis and of comprehension."

Higher education begins at the point where the accumulation of knowledge ceases to be the primary object of study, and discipline takes its place. This point is not within the sphere of ordinary public-school education; it lies between the grammar and high schools in large cities, or between the public schools and academies. Whoever labors to make the public schools do the work of academies, to make them schools of culture instead of schools for the teaching of useful knowledge, is an enemy to public-school education, and to the extent of his ability works an injury to the Commonwealth. The proportion of pupils in the lower grades of schools in the large cities of the United States, who enter the high schools, is exceedingly small. The great masses are not in circumstances that will admit of the pursuit of learning for purposes of culture; they attend school a few years in order to gain a knowledge of the elements of elocution, arithmetic, geography and penmanship, and enough practice to give facility in the use of such knowledge, then to work, to trades, to business, into the whirl and the toils of the life struggle, common to a very large proportion of the inhabitants of this country. Because of this necessity, inherited by most men, the purpose of the public-school course must ever be the acquisition of useful knowledge. In the processes of study and methods of instruction, it should be the aim of teachers in these schools to infuse lessons, both ethical and æsthetical, so as to inspire the souls of the young with a love for the good and the beautiful.

The profession of teaching requires the highest culture in its members, who, while instructing children in the elements of useful knowledge, may pour into the thirsting, capacious spirits of childhood copious draughts of living waters fresh from the fountain of perfect knowledge. Moral culture is not to be made the subject of occasional instruction. In the daily exercises of the school, in the conduct of teacher and pupils, in the illustrations of truths, the demonstrations of principles, the observations of facts and phenomena, in all places and at at all times, the spiritual growth of the pupils should be jealously guarded and affectionately encouraged. A sense of *personal spiritual worthiness* should be inculcated. Children of all ages and conditions in life should be taught to hold themselves in high respect, to do nothing that will invoke self-censure, or self-condemnation, the forerunners of degradation and debasement. Active, conscientious teaching may, in ways innumerable, scatter seeds of the good and the true, that will take root, and in the end come to a glorious fruition, culminating in moral and religious culture.

The few who pass into the city high schools and into the academies go there in order to enjoy the advantages of a disciplinary course of instruction, incompatible with the objects of the schools for the masses. The higher institutions must, therefore, if they are to satisfy the longings of those who enter them, provide ample facilities, in a skillfully-devised curriculum, for a disciplinary training that will give power and goodness as its resultant.

The science of language, pure mathematics, the philosophy of the mind and cosmology may properly find place in a disciplinary course of studies. Language, mathematics and science, in their numerous systems and combinations, present a series of subjects which can be studied in groups of three, so that the student will daily recite a lesson in language, in science and in mathematics. The curriculum of studies should be so constructed as to present only three studies to a student in each term. The Faculty should be so organized as to provide a teacher for each department of language and literature, mathematics, and philosophy. Whether in a high school, an academy, or college, no man is a mental *Briareus*, and he who attempts to teach classes in a wide range of diversified subjects will not teach anything thoroughly. A teacher, to be successful, must be a student; the higher the grade of institution in which he teaches, the more imperative the necessity for close application to study. A professor in a college, or academy, and a teacher in a high school, who is not a close student, no matter what his educational advantages have been, is at best a superficial, technical, narrow teacher, and *qualis magister, talis discipulus.*

CHAPTER XVII.

GOVERNMENT.

GOVERNMENT, as applied to individuals, is derived from two sources: the governing power is within and directs, or it is without and controls. Either men govern themselves, or they are governed by others. A man who governs himself is a positive element in the government of society; a man who does not govern himself is either a passive, or a negative element in the government of society. Those who do not govern themselves must be governed. To the self-governed belongs the right, and upon them is imposed the duty, of governing those who do not govern themselves. Laws have their origin in, and derive their force from that part of the population of the Commonwealth that is self-governing. It is they who establish, support and defend governments; it is they who enact just laws and mercifully enforce them. Where the population of any state is nearly equally divided between the self-governing and the non-self-governing citizens, the government will necessarily be unstable, but where the self-governing element largely predominates in the citizenship of any state, the government will be secure in its establishment, equitable in its provisions and just in its enforcement of laws. The training institutions of a government, therefore, should be so organized and conducted as to cultivate habits of self-government. A Commonwealth is strengthened and enriched by the growth of a self-governing population, but it is weakened and impoverished by the increase of a class of citizens that must be controlled, that must be constrained, that must be forced to obey righteous laws.

The public schools are institutions of the Commonwealth; in them the youth should be educated, not only in the elements of useful knowledge, but they should be trained in the exercise of their mental forces, so as to enable them to grow up useful, power-giving and wealth-producing citizens. The genius of the government of the Commonwealth should find an exemplification in the government of every school in that Commonwealth. It is not enough for the purposes of the state, that the schools shall be so governed as to maintain order and to enforce discipline. Order must be secured and discipline must be sustained, not through physical power, or the fear which arises from the apprehension of the exercise of the physical power possessed by the teacher, but they must be the result of a system of training that cultivates in the pupils habits of self-government.

A code of laws, or rules submitted for the government of a school is not very likely to secure permanent good. A more profitable method will be found in the explanation and application of a few of the simple fundamental rules of life—those principles which should govern the actions of men and their conduct toward others. Duty to self, duty to others, are texts upon which the teacher may enlarge until he is quite certain that their full force is understood and felt by all the pupils—how injury intended for others reverts upon self; how every act inconsistent with the highest duty to others reflects upon and debases the actor; how the happiness of children and of adults may be destroyed by selfishness, by covetousness, by prevarication, by falsehoods, by deceptions; how doing good to others ennobles one's self, expands one's power, enlarges the heart of the actor. "Therefore, all things whatsoever ye would that men should do to you, do ye even so to them: for this is the law and the prophets." This should be made the fundamental law, the constitution, o. every school government; it may be explained, illustrated and applied as circumstances arise in the conduct of school affairs.

These general suggestions are applicable to schools of all grades, and will differ only in methods of application, as the capacity and comprehension of the members of the school may indicate. In primary and mixed schools the teacher should, on the day of opening the term, and at proper intervals thereafter, explain in a general way the purposes for which the school is established, the objects for which pupils attend it. He may show how, by misconduct of any sort, these objects may be thwarted and the purpose defeated, and how, by the proper conduct of each pupil, the interests of all will be promoted. Every pupil comes to school to acquire knowledge; each individual should address himself to that work, and should recognize the fact, that all of his associates are there for the same purpose. Teachers are employed at considerable expense to the district, not to maintain order among the boys and girls, to govern them, but to teach them, to aid them in their efforts to accumulate knowledge. If, therefore, a teacher is required to devote a considerable portion of his time to enforcing discipline, the pupils will to that extent be defrauded of his services as an instructor and assistant in their labors.

Whenever, during the progress of the school, cases of infractions of good conduct occur, the teacher may avail himself of the opportunity to explain how such conduct affects the whole school, how it injures every member of that school, how it disturbs the general good order, how it interferes with the application of the mind to healthful study, how it exerts generally a demoralizing influence on the whole school. He thus shows that any member of the school guilty of such breach of order is in reality a public enemy, not only injuring himself, but injuring all his associates and companions; that he is not sinning against the teacher, but against his fellow-pupils. Then the moral force of the community is invoked to suppress unruliness. Those who govern themselves exert an influence over others far more keenly felt by the offender than any words, or chastisement, that could be inflicted by the teacher. There is a public sentiment in favor of good order, and whoever in the least violates good order in the school encounters that public sentiment, and is thereby rebuked.

A general system of government, based upon the self-governing elements in the schools, is preferable to a code of prescribed laws, for the reason that it cultivates habits of self-government in all the pupils and exhibits the force of that power, whenever a restraining influence is required to maintain order. Rules cannot be devised to meet every case of discipline required in school government. The circumstances that invoked the offence, the character of the offender, the general discipline of the school, the public sentiment in the neighborhood, the social status of the offending pupil, his health, his age, and many other considerations,—enter as important elements in the case, which the teacher is called upon to try and to determine and to punish. If laws are laid down, they must be enforced, or they invoke demoralization, yet it not unfrequently happens, that the enforcement of the law works a greater injury than its violation.

Teachers must be careful not to require too much of pupils, not to set up a Procrustean frame, to the length of which every pupil must be stretched or chopped. The inflexibility of rules and the flexibility of the self-governing system makes the latter eminently preferable, under circumstances where the largest variety of cases are most likely to arise, in the treatment of which love and mercy must always temper the administration of justice.

The doctrines of proper respect for the rights and conditions of others should be thoroughly inculcated. Whether in moving about the school-room, whether in passing in and out, whether in going to and returning from school, pupils should be instructed to so conduct themselves as to enjoy the largest liberty and the fullest freedom of conduct, compatible with a similar enjoyment of these rights and privileges by those with whom they are associated. Teachers must closely observe the conduct of their pupils in all the relations of school-day life, and wherever a breach of the general idea of equality of rights and the enjoyment of privileges occur, the proper remedy should be applied in such way as will direct the attention of the members of the school to the fact, that such conduct as calls forth rebuke is a trespass upon the rights and privileges of society. How these same principles are applicable to the affairs of life, teachers may frequently explain and illustrate. By a system of government thus derived and founded, morality is taught in the every-day life of the school-room, and a high degree of moral culture is secured, which v il ever manifest itself in the self-governing conduct of the pupils in every vicissitude of life.

CHAPTER XVIII.

BOOKS, MANUFACTURE AND SALE.

THE public good requires that the book question, as it affects the public schools, should be settled in the interests of the people. The rapacity of school-book publishers must be repressed. The corrupting influence of the trade as now practiced must be counteracted, and the character of the books to be used by the people must be radically improved. The frequent changes from one series of books to another, in all the branches taught in the public schools, has greatly increased the labor of school-directors, is embarrassing to teachers, expensive to parents and demoralizing to pupils. The chief abuse is found first, in the multiplication of books into an extended series on each common-school branch. This pernicious practice has grown out of the nature of the schools as they were a quarter of a century ago. There was then no classification; each pupil brought such book into school as he chanced to find at home, and prosecuted his studies as best he might alone. Thus, for example, an arithmetic of some forgotten author was used by a pupil, who sat at his desk solving such problems as he was able to, and applied to the teacher for solutions of those beyond his comprehension; all of these were transferred from the slate into the "sum-book." The pupils were in no case arranged in classes, so as to study arithmetic together, and never received explanations of the principles thereof from the teacher.

Similar methods obtained in the study of reading, geography and grammar; only two or three "readers" were in use; a history of the United States, some general history, the New Testament, or any miscellaneous book might be taken into school and read. Where two or more pupils happened to have the same book, they were placed in a class together. This was of old the uniform practice. The system of classifying the pupils in the public schools is of recent adoption; the advantages of the change are so universally admitted that it would be superfluous to present an argument here in its favor. In all schools, pupils of the same average capacity are now required to purchase the same books and to pursue their studies together. All that was formerly taught in the majority of the public schools was reading and arithmetic. In a few isolated cases, geography, or grammar was taught.

It will be seen, therefore, that pupils from the age of six years to sixteen, the usual school-years, were compelled to devote all of that period of ten important years to the study of two or three, or at most four, branches. Book publishers were quick to discover that here was occasion for the multiplication of books. Keeping a bright boy or girl on the subject of arithmetic for eight or ten years was a feat, not to be accomplished by the use of a single book; therefore the idea of a "primary," a "common-school" and a "higher arithmetic" was originated and speedily became a practical fact. The same observation may be made with reference to other public-school branches.

The subject of English grammar is served up in three books, the "Elementary," the "Common-school" and the "Analytic." Geography is diluted through a series of three or four books—the "Primary," the "Secondary," the "Common-school" and the "Comprehensive." Arithmetic has far outrun its original scope, and we now have "Mental," "Intellectual," "School Arithmetic" and "Higher Arithmetic."

The occasion for the multiplication of these books was not in any sense found in the subject of the sciences, but arose from the condition of the schools, which was taken advantage of by bookmakers and converted to their own profit. The extension of the subject of reading into a series of six or eight books is a scheme invented by, and solely for the benefit of those who are interested in making and selling books. As to arithmetic, the whole subject, as far as it is material and useful to teach it in the public schools, to the millions of boys and girls who frequent them, can be and should be treated in one small volume, and it would be so treated if the interests of the people alone were consulted.

The schools of the people have risen from the low and formative condition in which they were held thirty years ago. The whole system of instruction has been elevated, more is demanded in the way of elementary training, and more is given. Teaching, which was then deemed to be a servile vocation, has taken an honorable position, and is with forcible dignity asserting its claims to be ranked as one of the "learned professions." Teachers are respected because their intellectual attainments and their general culture and high social qualities command the esteem of the most refined circles of society. The public school is no longer a place wherein to gain a little facility in the art of reading, writing and ciphering, but an institution wherein to instruct the youth of the country in the elements of a liberal education.

The whole period of school-life is no longer to be devoted to the study of two or three simple branches, to which is attached a vulgar idea of utility. A number of sciences have been so simplified in their elements by the progress of investigation, that the essential truths of many of these can be successfully taught in our public schools. Thus has been simplified the science of botany, of anatomy and physiology, of natural philosophy, chemistry, geology and astronomy. There are educated teachers, who now find employment in school-rooms, able to teach these sciences, and to take classes through algebra, geometry and surveying. History, no longer used as a mere reading book, is now regularly taught as one of the most profitable studies in the school. Drawing, physical geography, the elements of mechanics, the principles of engineering, have been so reduced to system that they may with profit be introduced into the public schools. These new studies, pressing upon the attention of the pupil and demanding a place in the common schools, will repress the magnified importance heretofore given to reading, arithmetic, geography and grammar. These sciences are found to be more useful and more agreeable than those which they assail for room, and their influence on the minds of the pupils is more salutary and elevating. The common schools are for the education of the great millions in this country. There the pupils receive their educational training; comparatively few go beyond the elements of a common-school course.

It should be the aim of those who have in charge the arrangement of public-school education, to give to the children as large a store of facts in all the sciences as is possible, having regard to the age, comprehension and school-period of the pupil. Unquestionably, therefore, the system of bookmaking must be changed. We must go back to the original idea of treating subjects in the closest compass consistent with a fair elucidation of the principles, necessary to a comprehension of the science under consideration. Reading must be taught in the primer, speller and the reader. Arithmetic, "mental" and "written," must be compressed within the limits of one common-school book. The rules that are of use in the whole range of business transactions are few in number and simple in their character; these can be explained and illustrated in one small, convenient volume. The idea that books must be lumbered up with puzzling examples to weary the teacher, embarrass the pupil and consume time is one of those ancient absurdities, that the present generation must cast away. They were placed in our books in olden times because they served to discipline the mind, and because there was no system of physical sciences to take their places in the curriculum of studies. A more enlightened philosophy teaches us, that the acquisition of knowledge most effectually disciplines the mind, and the exploration of nature in the operations of science furnishes new fields wherein to reap rich harvests of soul-inspiring truths. The facts in science, and the philosophy which combines these facts into sciences, are more readily acquired and more easily comprehended than a confused and senseless jumble of figures, that illustrate processes useful only to discipline, and even in that sense no longer profitable exercises, when compared with the study of the natural sciences. The mind is not only to be disciplined, but it is to be stored with materials upon which to exercise its thinking powers. There is little danger that book-publishers will not be quick enough to scent this new condition of things in the public schools. Authors will be called upon to condense their numerous series into single volumes when the parent insists that he shall purchase the subject of arithmetic in one small, cheap book, and shall not be taxed with the expense of four or five. As soon as the pupil discovers that the subject may be mastered within a small compass, and as soon as the teacher resolves to carry his class into new fields of discovery, the majority of publishers will make haste to supply the demand. The onus of the work, therefore, necessary to break down this bungling system that is now in use, and of substituting one that is more in accordance with the wants of the times, rests rather with school men than with bookmakers.

A very pernicious practice, demoralizing teachers and pupils, increasing the expenses of education and corrupting the school authorities, is the system by which worthless school-books are frequently inflicted upon the public. Agents are employed at great expense and are sent out into all parts of the country to visit school-directors, to ply teachers and to labor by means, both honorable and dishonorable, to force the publications they represent into schools. It thus frequently happens that without any recommendation of superiority whatever, a series of books, including readers, copy-books, arithmetics, grammars and geographies, in use in a school-district, are thrown out and new books introduced. The parents are compelled to purchase books that are in no way superior—very often, indeed, not equal—in merit to those that they have laid aside. Frequently old books are purchased by the house that presents the new books; in other instances the new books are given gratuitously to those who have the old, but it must be apparent to every one possessed of the slightest knowledge of the laws of trade, that all this loss, this extraordinary expense, must finally be made up by the sale of these very books.

School-books, which might be furnished at small cost, are made expensive by the system that contributes so largely to demoralize school-officers. Book-publishers themselves have felt the full effects of these practices, and have labored by "boards of trade" and by private agreements to repress and abolish them, but all these efforts have hitherto failed. The people, therefore, must have recourse to legislation for their own protection, as well as for the protection of bookmakers and booksellers. The influence of normal schools, and the fact that teachers are interested in the elevation of the standard of qualification, tend to hasten the period, when the number of books to be used will be greatly reduced. Then the temptation to grasp and control a trade which has hitherto proven a prize so tempting as to demoralize and corrupt all who engaged in it will, to a great extent, be removed. The facts that are now set forth, and repeated through numerous combinations, in the most bungling manner, in order to multiply books, will be communicated directly and practically by the teacher, and the principles, which bind these facts into sciences, will be elaborated in convenient books. It is the province of normal schools and teachers to hasten this period, and when it arrives, part of the result will be, that the funds, now uselessly expended in the purchase of books, will be much more profitably employed in increasing the salaries of teachers, and in otherwise strengthening the forces, that tend to advance and perfect the system of schools and methods of instruction, supported by, and provided for the education of, all the people.

THE END.

In this system of Drawing the underlying principle is the effort to produce breadth and freedom of effect. For this purpose the multiplication of small figures and contracted lines (as in some systems of Drawing) is avoided, the figures being drawn large and bold, so as to give a freer sweep to the hand and cultivate greater accuracy in the eye of the student. By this means errors which in small figures could hardly be detected become magnified and readily observable, while the hand is trained to the production of vigorous effects, boldness being cultivated instead of minuteness.

Elementary Series.—The course of instruction comprised in this series is devoted to practice in the drawing of lines and the study of their natures and distinctions. These lines are combined into familiar forms, so as to render the exercises more attractive, while the shapes of leaves are given, in order to lead to a study of lines in Nature and promote that close observation of natural forms so essential to any true progress in art.

Plane Geometry.—This series gives the definitions of terms, which should be separately studied, and the answers to the questions illustrated on the blackboard by the formation of the leading geometrical figures. The lines in these illustrations should be made at least a foot in length and drawn sharp and clear with one stroke of the hand. This is for use in the Primary Department of schools.

Architectural Series embraces the application of the principles taught in the preceding books, and is also adapted to be taken up by those whose advanced instruction enables them to dispense with the Elementary studies. It leads, by a graduated succession of exercises, to the ready formation of architectural forms. Great attention is also paid to instruction in the various terms employed in Architecture, and exact definitions of these terms are given, so as to yield a thorough acquaintance with the subject.

Perspective Series is one of the most important in the course, a knowledge of the principles of Perspective being absolutely essential as a basis of the art of Drawing. Special care is taken to give the student a comprehension of the principles of this branch of art-study, since, without properly understanding it, no useful progress can be made.

Ornamentation.—The series on Ornament is also highly important, as a knowledge of the principles of ornamental design forms the proper foundation for the production of original art-work. The study of Decorative Art needs to be preceded by some acquaintance with the classic styles, in which the outlines and groupings of Nature are conventionally treated and reduced to that strict symmetry and well-balanced repetition so requisite to effect in this branch of art. The elements of the Egyptian, Greek, Roman, and other ancient styles are taught, and their application to modern ideas of ornamentation is practically shown.

Object-Drawing.—A series devoted to Object-Teaching, in which the principles of Perspective and the use of Light and Shade are practically applied in the drawing of simple geometrical forms and other familiar objects, full directions being given as to the methods necessary to be employed in reproducing such forms.

Landscape.—The system closes with a series devoted to Landscape studies, in which is embraced the final application of all the preceding exercises, the student being taught how to reproduce the effects of outer Nature and prepared to seek his subjects in the great art-studio of the field and the forest, and also to successfully imitate some of Nature's countless beauties of outline, form and grouping.

Easy Drawing Lessons.—A series of Card exercises designed for children's practice on Slate or Blackboard, previous to the use of a Drawing-Book.

www.ingramcontent.com/pod-product-compliance
Lightning Source LLC
LaVergne TN
LVHW020212110826
845151LV00003B/690

* 9 7 8 1 4 2 5 5 3 3 7 2 4 *